Dave Ranney, or, Thirty Years on the Bowery

Dave Ranney

GW01393114

DODO PRESS

DAVE RANNEY

OR THIRTY YEARS ON THE BOWERY

DAVE RANNEY

OR

THIRTY YEARS ON THE BOWERY

An Autobiography

Introduction by Rev. A. F. Schauffler, D. D.

1910

This story of my life is dedicated to

DR. A. F. SCHAUFFLER

Who stuck by me through thick and thin

Honest endeavor is ne'er thrown away;
God gathers the failures day by day,
And weaves them into His perfect plan
In ways that are not for us to scan.
—*Lucy Whittemore Myrick, 1876.*

INTRODUCTION

The autobiography which this book contains is that of a man who through the wonderful dealings of Providence has had a most remarkable experience. I have known the writer for about seventeen years, and always most favorably. For a number of years past he has been Bowery Missionary for the New York City Mission and Tract Society, and has shown himself faithful, capable and conscientious. His story simply illustrates how the gospel of the grace of God can go down as far as man can fall, and can uplift, purify, and beautify that which was degraded and "well nigh unto cursing."

As a testimony as to what God can work, and how He can transform a man from being a curse to himself and to the world into being a blessing, the story is certainly fascinating, and ought to encourage any who have lost hope to turn to Him who alone is able to save. It ought also to encourage all workers for the downfallen to realize that God is able to save unto the uttermost all who come to Him through Jesus Christ, the all-sufficient Saviour.

With confidence I recommend this book to those who are interested in the rescue of the fallen, knowing that they will praise God for what has been wrought and will trust Him for future wonderful redemptions.

A. F. SCHAUFFLER.

New York City.

CONTENTS

"Let me live in a house by the side of the road,
Where the race of men go by.
Men that are good and
* men that are bad, as good and*
*   as bad as I.*
I would not sit in the scorner's seat,
Nor hurl the cynic's ban.
Let me live in a house by the side of the road
And be a friend to man."

CHAPTER I

BOYHOOD DAYS

I have often been asked the question, "Why don't you write a book?" And I have said, "What is the use? What good will it do?" I have thought about it time and time again, and have come to the conclusion to write a story of my life, the good and the bad, and if the story will be a help, and check some one that's just going wrong, set him thinking, and point him on the right road, praise God!

I was born in Hudson City, N. J., over forty years ago, when there were not as many houses in that town as there are now. I was born in old Dutch Row, now called Beacon Avenue, in a two-story frame house. In those days there was an Irish Row and a Dutch Row. The Irish lived by themselves, and the Dutch by themselves.

Quite frequently the boys of the two colonies would have a battle royal, and there would be things doing. Sometimes the Dutch would win out, sometimes the Irish, and many's the time there was a cut head and other bruises. Sometimes a prisoner would be taken, and then we would play Indian with him, and do everything with him except burn him. We were all boys born in America, but if we lived in Dutch Row, why, we had to be Dutch; but if, on the other hand, we happened to live in Irish Row, we had to be Irish. I remember moving one time to Irish Row, and I wondered what would happen when I went to play with the old crowd. They said, "Go and stay with the Irish." I did not know what to do. I would not fight my old comrades, so I was neutral and fought with neither.

We had a good many ring battles in those days, and many's the fight we had without gloves, and many's the black eye I got, and also gave a few. I believe nothing does a boy or girl so much good as lots of play in the open air. I never had a serious sickness in my life except the measles, and that was easy, for I was up before the doctor said I ought to get out of bed. Those were happy days, and little did I think then that I would become the hard man I turned out to be.

1

I had a good Christian mother, one who loved her boy and thought there was nothing too good for him, and I could always jolly her into getting me anything I wanted. God bless the mothers! How true the saying is, "A boy's best friend is his mother." My father I won't say so much about. He was a rough man who loved his cups, and died, as you might say, a young man through his own waywardness. I did love my mother, and would give anything now to have her here with me as I am writing this story. She has gone to heaven, and I was the means of sending her to an early grave through my wrong-doings. She did not live to see her boy saved. Many's the time I would promise her to lead a different life, and I meant it too, but after all I could not give up my evil ways.

THE FIRST TASTE FOR DRINK

I remember when I first acquired the taste for drink. My grandfather lived with us, and he liked his mixed ale and would send me for a pint two or three times a day. In those days the beer was weighed so many pounds to the quart. Every time I went for the beer I used to take a swallow before I came back, and sometimes two, and after a while I really began to enjoy it. Do you know, I was laying the foundation right there and then for being what I turned out to be—a drunkard. I remember one time—yes, lots of times—that I was under the influence of the vile stuff when I was not more than ten years of age.

I received a public school education. My school-days were grand good days. I had all the sport that comes to any boy going to school. I would rather play ball than go home to dinner. In those days the game was different from what it is at the present time. I was up in all athletic sports when I was a boy. I could jump three quick jumps and go twenty-eight and a half feet; that was considered great for a schoolboy.

There was one game I really did enjoy; the name of it was "How many miles?" It is played something like this: You choose sides, and it doesn't matter how many there are on a side. Of course each side would be eager to get the quickest and fastest runner on their side. How I did like that game! We then tossed to see who would be the outs and who would chase the outs, and many's the mile we boys would run. We would be late for school and would be kept in after three o'clock; that would break my heart, but I would forget all about it the next day and do the same thing again.

Our teacher, J. W. Wakeman—God bless him!—is living yet, and I hope he will live a good many years more. A boy doesn't always like his teacher, and I was no exception; I did not like him very much. He gave me more whippings than any other boy in the school. All the learning I received was, you might say, pounded into me. He used to say to me, "David, why don't you be good and study your lessons? There is the making of a man in you, but if you don't study you will be fit for nothing else than the pick and shovel." How those words rang in my ears many a time in after years when they came true, when I had to use the pick and shovel! I am not saying anything against that sort of labor; it has its place. We must fill in somewhere, in some groove, but that was not mine.

How I did enjoy in after years, when I was roaming over the world, thinking of my old schoolmates! I could name over a dozen who were filling positions of trust in their own city; lawyers, surrogates, judges, and some in business for themselves, making a name and doing something, while I was no earthly use to myself or to any one else. Some people say, "Such is life; as you make your bed so you must lie." How true it was in my case! I made my bed and had to lie on it, but I can truthfully say I did not enjoy it.

There are many men that are down and out now who had a chance to be splendid men. They are now on the Bowery "carrying the banner"—which means walking the streets without a place to call home—without food or shelter, but they could, if they looked back to their early life, see that they were making their beds then, or as the Bible reads, sowing the seed. Listen, young people, and take heed. Don't believe the saying, "A fellow must sow his wild oats." The truth is just this: as you sow so shall you reap. I was sowing when I was drinking out of the pail of beer, and I surely did reap the drunkard's portion—misery.

A TRUANT

I was a great hand at playing hookey—that is, staying away from school and not telling your parents. I would start for school in the morning, but instead of going would meet a couple of boys and we would hide our books until closing-time. If any boy was sent to my home with a note, I would see that boy and tell him if he went he knew what he would get. He knew it meant a good punching, and he would not go. I would write a note so that the boy could take it back to the teacher saying that I was sick and would be at school when I got better.

I remember how I was found out one time. We met as usual—the hookey-players, I mean—and started down to the Hackensack River to have a good day. Little did I know what would happen before the day was over. One of the boys with us went out beyond his depth and was drowned. I can still hear his cries and see his face as he sank for the last lime. We all could swim a little, and we tried our best to save him, but his time had come.

That wound up his hookey-playing, and you would think it would make me stop too; but no, I went right along sowing the seed, and planting it good and deep for the Devil.

I recollect the first time I went away from home. It happened this way: The teacher got tired of receiving notes saying I was sick, and she determined to see for herself—for I had a lady for teacher in that class—what the trouble was.

One afternoon whom should I see coming in the gate but my teacher, and now I was in a fix for fair. I knew if she saw mother it was all up with me, so I ran and met her and told her mother was out and would not be back until late. She asked me how I was getting on. I said I was better and would be at school in the morning. She said, "I am glad of that."

When she turned to go I could have flung my cap in the air and shouted. I thought I had fooled her and could go on playing hookey, but you know the old adage, "There's many a slip." Just at this time my mother looked out of the window and asked who was there and what she wanted. Well, mother came down, and things were made straight as far as she and the teacher were concerned; but I was in for it; I knew that by the way mother looked at me. The jig was up, I was found out, and I knew things would happen; and I did not want to be around when mother said, "You just wait!" I knew what that meant, so I determined to go out into the world and make my own way.

I was a little over thirteen years of age, and you know a boy does not know much at that age, but I thought I did. I went over the fence with mother after me. If dad had been home I guess he could have caught me, that is if he had been sober. Mother could not run very fast, so I got clear of the whip for that time at least. I got a good distance from the house and then I sat down to think. I knew if I went home a whipping was waiting for me, and that I could do without.

There was a boy just a little older than myself, Mike — —,[1] that was "on the bum," as we used to say. The boys would give him some of the lunch they had brought to school, and I thought I would join forces with and be his pal. I saw Mike and told him all about the licking, and Mike said, "Don't go home; you are a fool if you do." We went around, and I was getting hungry, when we thought of a plan by which we could get something to eat. Mother ran a book in a grocery store, and Mike said, "Go to the store and get a few things, and say you don't have the book but will bring it when you come again." I went to the store and got a ham, a pound of butter, two loaves of bread and one box of sardines.

[1] Where proper names are left blank they refer to real persons or places.

Some people will ask how I can remember so many years back. I remember my first night away from home as though it was yesterday, and I'll never forget it as long as I live. After I got the things the grocer said, "Where is the book?" I told him mother had mislaid it, and he said, "Bring it the next time." We built a fire and cooked the ham and had lots to eat.

Up to this time it had all been smooth sailing; it was warm and we had a good time in general. We had a swim with some other boys, and after telling them not to say that they saw me, we left them. I asked Mike where we were going to sleep, and he said, "I'll show you when it's time."

After a while Mike said, "I guess we had better go to bed." Off we started across the lots until we came to a big haystack, and Mike stooped down and began to pull hay out of the stack and work his way inside. Remember I was green at the business; I had never been away from home before; and Mike, though only a little older, was used to this kind of life. Well, I pulled out hay enough, as I thought, and crawled in, but there was no sleep for me. I kept thinking and thinking. I would call Mike and ask him if he was asleep, and he would say, "Oh, shut up and let a fellow sleep!"

I am no coward, never was, but I was scared that night for fair. About midnight I must have dozed off to sleep when something seemed to be pushing at my feet. I was wide awake now, and shook Mike, but he only turned over and seemed to sleep all the sounder. I could hear the grunting and pushing outside all the time. My head was under and my feet covered with the hay, when something took hold of my foot and began to chew. My hair stood on end, and I gave a yell that would have awakened "The Seven Sleepers." It woke Mike, and the last I heard of him that night he was laughing as though he would split his sides, and all he could shout was, "Pigs, pigs!" as I went flying toward home. I got there as soon as my feet would carry me. I found the house up and mother and sister crying, while father was trying to make them stop. When I shook the door it opened and I was home again, and I was mighty glad.

The reason for the crying was that when it got late and the folks began to look for me, one of the boys said that the last time he saw me I was swimming with Mike — —. When I did not come home they thought surely I was drowned, but I was born for a different fate. Sometimes in my years of roaming afterwards I wished I had been drowned as they thought. They were so glad to see me again that there was no whipping, and I went to school next morning promising to be a better boy.

A BASEBALL GAME

I was fast becoming initiated in the ways of the Devil. There was nothing that I would not do. I remember one time when mother thought I was going to school but found out I was "on the hook." She decided to punish me, and that night after I had gone to sleep she came into my room and took all my clothes except my shirt. I certainly was in a fix. I had to catch for my team and I would not miss that game of ball for anything in the world; I simply had to go. In looking around the room I found a skirt belonging to my sister that I thought would answer my purpose. I had my shirt on and I put the skirt on over my head. Then I ripped the skirt up the center and tied it around each leg with a piece of cord—anything for that game!—and there I was with a pair of trousers manufactured out of a girl's skirt. But I had to catch that game of ball that day at any cost. Getting to the ground was easy. I opened the window and let myself down as far as I could and then dropped. I arrived all right, a little shaken up, but what is that to a boy who has a ball game in his head!

I got to the game all right and some of the boys fixed me up. I don't remember which side won that game, but when it was finished I went home and met mother, and the interview was not a pleasant one, though she did not give me a whipping.

I used to read novels, any number of them, in those days—all about Indians, pirates, and all those blood-and-thunder tales—lies. You can not get any good out of them, and they do corrupt your mind. I would advise the young people who read these lines, and older folks also, if this is your style of reading, to stop right where you are. Get some good books—there are plenty of them—and don't fill your mind with stuff that only unfits you for the real life of the years to come.

A NOON SHOP MEETING ADDRESSED
BY MR. RANNEY.

CHAPTER II

FIRST STEPS IN CRIME

I was getting tired of school and wanted to go to work. I had a good Christian man for my Sunday-school teacher, Mr. M., a fairly rich man, and I did think a good deal of him. I liked to go to Sunday-school and was often the first in my class. The teacher would put up a prize for the one that was there first. Sometimes it would be a baseball bat, skates, book, or knife. I would let myself out then and would be first and get the prize.

I asked Mr. M. to get me work in an office. After a few weeks he called and told my mother he had got me a job in Jersey City, in the office of a civil engineer, at $3 a week. I was a happy boy as I started in on my first day's work. It was easy; all I had to do was to open up and dust the office at 8 A. M., and close at 5 P. M. I used to run errands and draw a little. But after a few weeks the newness of work wore off and I wished I was back at school again, where I could play hookey and have fun with the other fellows.

THE FIRST THEFTS

I had lots of time on my hands, and you know the saying, "Satan finds some mischief still for idle hands to do." He certainly found plenty for me. The boss was a great smoker and bought his cigars by the box. He asked me if I smoked, and I said no, for I had not begun to smoke as yet. Well, he left the box of cigars around, always open, so I thought I would try one, and I took a couple out of the box. See how the Devil works with a fellow. He seemed to say, "Now if you take them from the top he will miss them," so he showed me how to take them from the bottom. I took out the cigars that were on top, and when I got to the bottom of the box I crossed a couple and took the cigars, and you could not tell that any had been taken out. That was the beginning of my stealing. The cigars were not missed, and I thought how easy it was, but this beginning proved to be just a stepping-stone to what followed.

I did not smoke the cigars then, but waited until I got home. After supper I went out and met Mike — —, and gave him one of them, and I started in to smoke my first cigar. Mike could smoke and not get sick, but there never was a sicker boy than I was. I thought I was going to die then and there and I said, "No more cigars for me." I recovered, however, and as usual forgot my good resolutions. That turned out to be the beginning of my smoking habit, and I was a good judge of a cigar when I was but fourteen years of age. I went on stealing them until the boss tumbled that some one was taking them and locked them up for safe keeping. I never smoked a cigarette in all my life. I know it takes away a young fellow's brains and I really class cigarettes next to drink and would warn boys never to smoke them.

I had been in the office now about three months. At the end of each month I received a check for $12. It seemed a fortune to me and I hated to give it in at the house. The third month I received the check as usual, made out to bearer. Well, I went home and gave the check to mother, and she said I was a good boy and gave me fifty cents to spend.

I watched my mother and saw her put the check in an unused pitcher in the closet on the top shelf. It seemed as though some one was beside me all the time telling me to take it and have a good time. It belonged to me and no one else had a right to it, Satan seemed to say. And what a good time I could have with it! They would never suspect me of taking it, and I could have it cashed and no one would ever know.

So I got up in the middle of the night and started right there and then to be a burglar. I went on tiptoe as softly as I could, and was right in the middle of the kitchen floor when I stumbled over a little stool and it made a noise. It was not much of a noise, but to me it seemed like the shot out of a cannon. I thought it would wake up the whole house, but nobody but mother woke, and she said, "Who's there?" I said nothing, only stood still and waited for her to fall asleep again. As I stood there a voice—and surely it was the voice of God—seemed to say, "Go back to bed and leave the check alone. It is not yours: it belongs to your mother. She is feeding and keeping you, and you are doing wrong." I think if the Devil had not butted in I would have gone to bed, but he said, "Now you are here no one sees you, and what a good time you can have with that check!" That settled all good thoughts and I went up to the closet, put my hand in the pitcher, took the check and went back to bed. That was my first burglary.

Did I sleep? Well, I guess not! I rolled and tossed all the balance of the night. I knew I had done wrong. But you see the Devil was there, and I really think he owned me from the time I stole the cigars—"that little beginning."

I got up the next morning, ate my breakfast and went to work. I still had the check, and all I had to do was to go to the bank and get it cashed. But I was afraid, and how I wished that the check was safe in the old pitcher. I worried all that day, and I think if I had gotten a chance that night after I got home, I would have put the check back. But the old Devil was there saying, "You fool, keep it! It is not missed, and even if it is no one will accuse you of stealing your own money." I tell you, the Devil had me hand and foot, and there seemed to be no getting away. Oh! if I could have had some person to tell me plainly what to do at this time, it might have been the turning-point in my life! Anyway, the check didn't get back to the pitcher. I had it and the Devil had me.

Next day I disguised myself somewhat. I made my face dirty and put on a cap. I had been wearing a hat before, so I thought the teller at the bank would not know me. I had been there often with checks for my boss. Well, the teller just looked at the check, gave me a glance, and passed out the $12. It did not take me long to get out of the bank. I knew I had done wrong, and I felt it, and would have given anything if I could have undone it; but it was too late, and my old companion, the Devil, said, "What a nice time you can have, and wasn't it easy!"

When I went home the first question was, "Did you see your check?" My dear mother asked me that, never thinking that her boy had taken it. Oh! if I had had the courage to tell her then and there, how much misery and trouble it would have saved me in after life! But I was a moral coward, and I said, "No, mother; where did you put it?" I had her guessing whether she really put it in the pitcher or not.

There was a regular hunt for that check, and I hunted as much as any one, but it could not be found. Mother did not know much about banks in those days, but some one told her about a week after that she ought to go to the bank and stop payment on the check. That sounded good to mother, and she said, "Dave, you and I will go to the bank and stop payment on that check." I was in it for fair this time. The only chance I had was in the teller not recognizing me.

We went to the bank, and mother told the teller about the lost— stolen—check, and for him to see that it wasn't paid. He said, "All right, madam, I'll not pay it if it is not already paid." He looked over the books and brought back the lost check. I had stood in the background all this time. Then my mother asked him whom he paid it to. He said it was hard for him to recall just then, "But I think I paid it to a boy," he said. "Yes, it was a boy, for I recollect that he had as dirty a face and hands as ever I saw." Mother pulled me up in front of him and told him to look at me and see if I was the boy. He looked at me for a minute or so—it seemed to me like an hour—then said, "No, that is not the boy that cashed the check, nothing like him. I am sure I should know that boy." In after years, when I was lined up in front of detectives for identification for some crime, identified or not, I always thought of a dirty face being a good disguise.

On the way home from the bank mother asked me all sorts of questions about boys I knew; if they had dirty faces and so on, but I did not know any such boys, so the check business died out. She little thought that her own boy was the thief, and she blamed my cousin, who was boarding with us at the time.

My grandfather was still with us, and he had quite a sum of money saved. He wanted some money, and he and I went to the bank and he drew out fifty dollars in gold. There was a premium on gold at that time, and he received two twenty-dollar gold-pieces and one ten. Well, that night he lost one of the twenty-dollar gold-pieces and never found it. There was a hot time the next morning, for he was sure he had it when he went to bed. My father was blamed for that, so you see the innocent suffer for the guilty.

I had quite a time with the money while it lasted, went out to the old Bowery Theatre, and had a good time in general. I little thought then that in after years I would be sitting on the old Bowery steps, down and out, without a cent in my pocket and without a friend in the world.

LOSING A POSITION

I was a boy of fourteen at this time, working in a civil engineer's office for three dollars per week, but I knew, young as I was, that as a profession engineering was not for me. I knew that to take it up I needed a good education, and that I did not have. I didn't like the trade, anyway, and didn't care whether I worked or not. That is the reason I lost my job.

One afternoon my employer sent me up Newark Avenue for a suit of clothes that had been made to order. He told me to get them and bring them back as soon as I could. I must say right here that my employer was a good man, and he took quite a liking to me. Many a time he told me he would make a great engineer out of me. I often look back and ask myself the question, "Did I miss my vocation?" And then there comes a voice, which I recognize as God's, saying, "You had to go through all this in order to help others with the same temptations and the same sins," and I say, "Amen."

After getting the clothes I went back to the building where I worked—No. 9 Exchange Place, Jersey City—and found the door locked. I waited around for a while, for I thought my employer wanted his clothes or he would not have sent me for them. Finally I got tired of waiting, and after trying the door once more and finding it still locked, I said to myself, "I'll just put these clothes in the furniture store next door and I'll get them to-morrow morning." I left them and told the man I would call for them in the morning, and started for home.

I was in bed dreaming of Indians and other things, when mother wakened me, shouting, "Where's the man's clothes?" I couldn't make out at first what all the racket was about. Then I heard men's voices talking in the yard, and recognized Mr. M., my Sunday-school teacher, and my employer, the man that was going to make a great engineer out of me. I went out on the porch and told him what I had done with the clothes, and he nearly collapsed. He was very angry, and drove off, saying, "You come to the office and get what's due you in the morning." I went the next morning, got my money, and bade him good-by. That was the last of my becoming one of the great engineers of the day.

I was glad, and I went back to school determined to study real hard, and I did remain in school for a year. Then the old craze for work came on me again. Father had died in the meantime, and mother was left to do the best she could, and I got a job with the determination to be a help to her.

AT WORK AGAIN

I got a position as office boy at 40 Broadway, then one of New York's largest buildings. The man I worked for was a commission merchant, a Hebrew, and one of the finest men I ever met in my life. He took me into his private office and we had a long talk, a sort of fatherly talk, as he had sons and daughters of his own. I loved that man. I had been brought up among the Dutch and Irish, and had never associated with the Jews, and I supposed from what I had heard that they were put on earth for us to get the best of, fire stones at, and treat as meanly as we could. That was my idea of a Jew—my boy idea. Yet here was a man, a Jew, one of the whitest men I ever met, who by his life changed completely my opinion of the Jews, and I put them down from that day as being pretty good people.

My mother did some work for his wife, and when he heard that I wanted to go to work he told her to send me over to his place of business, and that is how I got my second position in this big world.

I went to work with the determination to make a man of myself, and mother said:

"Now, Dave, be a good boy, and one of these days you will be a big merchant and I shall be proud of you." That was what I might have been if I had had the grace of God to make my life true. I am acquainted with some men to-day that started about the same time I did. They were boys that looked ahead, studied and went up step by step, and are to-day some of the best-known bankers in America.

They say "Hell is paved with good intentions," and I believe it is. We start out in life with the best intentions, but before we know it we are up against some temptation, and unless we have God with us we are sure to fall, and when we fall, why, it's the hardest thing in the world to get back where we tumbled from. I only wish I had taken the Saviour as my helper years ago. Oh! what a change He did make in my life after I did accept Him, seventeen years ago!

I started in to work at four dollars a week, and, as I said, I intended to be a great merchant. I meant well, if that was any consolation. My duties were to go to the postoffice and bring the mail, copy the letters, and run errands, and I was happy.

I was out one day on an errand, when whom should I meet but my old friend Mike — —, my chum of the pig incident. He said, "Hello, Dave, where are you working?" He had a job in a factory in Maiden Lane, at the same wages I was getting. I hadn't seen much of Mike lately, and to tell the truth I didn't care so much about meeting him. I am not superstitious by any means, but I really thought he was my Jonah. We talked a while, and we promised to meet and go home together. Like a foolish boy, I met him that night and many a time after.

TOUCH NOT, TASTE NOT

Mike was just learning to play pool, and one evening we had to go in and play a game. That night I had the first glass of beer I ever took in a saloon. Mike was getting to be quite a tippler, and he said, "Let's have a drink." I said I didn't want any, and I didn't. But he said—I really think the Devil was using Mike to make me drink—"Oh, be a man! One glass won't hurt you; it will do you good." And he talked to me about mother's apron-strings, and finally I took my first drink outside of what I drank when grandfather used to send me for beer.

15

Do you know, as I stood there before the bar, with that beer in my hand, I heard a voice just as plain as I ever heard anything, saying, "Don't take that stuff; it's no good, and will bring you to shame and misery. It will spoil your future, and you will never become the great merchant you started out to be. Put it down and don't drink it." That was twenty-five years ago, and many a time I have heard that voice since. How I wish now that I had listened to that voice and never taken that first drink! It is not the second or the one hundred and second drink that makes a man a drunkard, but the first.

I started to put the glass down, and with that Mike began to laugh, and his laugh brought the other fellows around. Of course Mike told them I was a milk-and-water boy. I could not stand it to be laughed at, so I put the glass of beer to my lips, swallowed it, and never made a face about it. Then the fellows said, "You're all right! You are initiated now and you're a man!"

I didn't feel very much like a man. I felt as though I was some fellow without a single spark of manhood in my whole make-up. I thought of mother; what would she say if she knew I had broken my promise to her? I had promised her when father died never to take a drink in all my life. I knelt at her dear side, with her hands upon my head, and she prayed that God would bless her boy and keep him from drink. I had honestly intended to keep that promise, but you see how the Devil popped in and once more made me do what I knew was wrong—drink that first cursed glass of beer.

I went home, walking all the way, and trying to get the smell out of my mouth. I could not face my dear mother, so I went to my room without supper. I thought that all she had to do was to look in my face and she would know that I had broken my promise, and I was ashamed. She came up later and asked me what was the matter, and I said I had a headache. If I had had the courage to tell her then, things might have been different! She brought me a cup of tea and bade me good-night.

The next night the Devil steered me into the same saloon. I drank again and again, till finally I could drink as much as any man, and it would take a good deal to knock me out.

I was still working for the merchant on Broadway, and my prospects were of the brightest. They all liked me and gave me a raise in salary, so I was now getting five dollars a week. But, you see, I was spending money on pool and drink, and five dollars didn't go so very far, so I began to steal. I had charge of the stamps—the firm used a great many—-and I had the mailing of all the letters. I would take out fifty cents from the money and balance the account by letters mailed. I began in a small way, and the Devil in me said, "How easy! You're all right." So I went on until I was stealing on an average of $1.50 per day. I still kept on drinking and playing cards. I had by this time blossomed out as quite a poker player and could do as many tricks as the best of them. I used to stay out quite late, and would tell mother that I was kept at the office, and little did she think that her only son was a gambler!

The Bible says, "Be sure your sin will find you out," and it proved true in my case. One night I was out gambling, and had had quite some luck. The fellows got to drinking, and in fact I got drunk, and when I started for home I could hardly walk. I fell down several times, when who should come along but mother and sister, and when they saw me staggering along they were astonished. I heard my mother say, "Oh! my God, my boy, my only son, oh! what happened to you?" Mother knew without asking what the matter was. She had often seen father reeling home under the influence of drink. But here was something she could not understand. Here was her only son beastly drunk, and she cried bitter tears. She took hold of one arm and my sister the other, and we finally reached home. I was getting pretty well sobered up by this time, and knew I was in for a lecture. My mother hadn't whipped me of late, but I dreaded her talk, and then I wished I had never met Mike ——.

Mother didn't say anything until we got home. She put me to bed, brushed my clothes, and told me to go to sleep. About two o'clock I woke up. There was mother kneeling by my bedside, praying God to save her boy and keep him from following in his father's footsteps. I lay there and listened and said amen to everything she asked God to do. Finally I could stand it no longer; I jumped out of bed and knelt beside my mother and asked God to forgive me. I threw my arms around mother's neck and asked her to forgive her boy, which she did. I determined right then and there to do better and never to drink any more.

I really meant to start all over again, but I didn't take Jesus with me—in fact, I think the Devil owned me for fair. I was pretty good for about a month, kept away from Mike and the other fellows, and mother was delighted. But this did not continue long; I met Mike again, and fell into the same groove, and was even worse than before.

Barnum was running his circus in New York then, and Mike and I decided to see the show and took a day off to go. I had not got leave of absence from work, so on our way home we planned what we could tell our bosses when we went to work the next morning.

When my employer came in that morning I told him I was sick the day before and not able to get out of bed. He just stood there and looked at me, and said, "What a liar you are! You were seen at the circus yesterday! Now, why didn't you tell me the truth, and I would have overlooked it? I can't have any one in my employ that I can't trust." So I had to look for another job. I was sorry, but it was my own fault. There I was, without a job and without a recommendation. What was I going to do? Surely "the way of the transgressor is hard."

I tell the men in the Mission night after night that I would rather deal with a thief than a liar, because you can protect yourself against a thief, but a liar—what can't a liar do? If I had only told the truth to my employer that day, why, as mother said afterwards, he would have given me a lecture, and it would have been all over.

DEEPER IN THE MIRE

Now what was I to tell my mother? You see, if you tell one lie you are bound to tell others, and after you have lied once, how easy it is! My side partner, the Devil, was there by my side to help me, and he said, "Don't tell your mother." So I said nothing, and took my carfare and lunch money every day, went out as if I were going to work, and hoped that something would turn up. That's the way with the sinners; they are always hoping and never doing. So it was with me, always hoping, and the Devil always saying, "Don't worry; it will be all right."

I used to dread going home at night and meeting my mother, and when she would say, "How have you got on to-day?" I was always ready with another lie, telling her I was doing finely, that the boss said he was going to give me a raise soon. He had—he had raised me right out of the place!

A BACK YARD ON THE BOWERY.

I was getting deeper and deeper into difficulty and could not see my way out. Oh! if I had only told my mother the truth, how different my life might have been! Saturday night was coming, and I did not have any money to bring home, and I did not know what to do. I thought of everything, but could not see my way out, when the thought came to me, "Steal!" My sister was saving up some money to buy a suit, and I knew where she kept it and determined to get it.

That night I entered her room and took all the money she had saved. No one saw me but God, but the Devil was there with me, and said, "Isn't it easy? Don't be a coward! God doesn't care." I knew right down in my heart that He did care, and in after years when I was wandering all over the States I found out how much He really cared, and I said, "Praise His name!"

ONE OF RANNEY'S FORMER HAUNTS.

CHAPTER III

INTO THE DEPTHS

After I had taken this money from my sister I knew that I was suspected. I was accused of taking it, but I was getting hardened; I had lost my job through lying; I was getting tired of home; I didn't care very much how things went.

About this time my elder sister was married and moved to New York. Her husband was a mechanic and made good money. He liked me, and when the theft was discovered I went and put up with him, staying there until I made money enough to leave, then I got out. All this time I was going from bad to worse, my associates being thieves and crooks and gamblers.

I shall never forget the first time I was arrested. I was with a hardened crook, and we had made a haul of some hundred dollars. But as luck would have it we were caught and sent away for nine months on a "technicality." If we had received our just dues the lowest term would have been five years each. I thought my time in prison would never come to an end, but it did at last, and I was free. But where was I to go? My mother had moved to New York to be near my sister, so I went and called on them. Mother asked me where I had been. I made some kind of an excuse, but I could see by mother's eye that she did not take much stock in it.

I remained at home, and finally got work in a fruit house on Washington Street, at eight dollars a week. I was quite steady for a while, and mother still had hopes of her boy. But through the same old company and drink I lost that job.

MARRIAGE

About this time I ran across a girl who I thought would make a good wife, and we were married. I was then in the crockery business in a small way, and if I had stuck to business I should be worth something now. I'll never forget the day of the wedding. The saying is, "Happy is the bride the sun shines on," but there was no sunshine that day. It rained, it simply poured. Mother tried to get the girl to throw me over; she told her I would never make her a good husband; and I guess Mary was sorry afterward that she did not take her advice.

The night of the wedding we had quite a blowout, and I was as drunk as I could be. I'd ring in right here a bit of advice to my girl readers: Don't ever try to convert a man—I mean one who drinks— by marrying him, for in ninety-nine cases out of a hundred you won't succeed. In my case I was young and did not care how the wind blew. I stayed out nights and neglected my home, but I must say, bad as I was, I never hit my wife. I think any man that raises his hand to hit a woman is worse than a cur, and that he will certainly be punished in some way for it.

Things went from bad to worse, and one day I came home to the store and there was no wife. She had gone. Married and deserted in two months! I felt sore, and all I thought about was to get even with my wife. I sold out the business, got a couple hundred dollars together, and started after her. I found out that she had gone to Oswego, and I sent her a telegram and was met at the station by her brother. It did not take me long to get next to him. In a very short time I had him thinking there was no one like Ranney. Mary and I made up and I promised never to drink again, and we started for New York. My promises were easily broken, for before we got to Syracuse both her brother and I were pretty drunk.

After reaching New York we went to mother's house and stayed there until we got rooms, which we did in a few days. Mary's brother got work in a lumberyard. I hunted as usual for a job, praying I wouldn't get it. I went hustling lumber and worked two days, leaving because it took the skin off my hands. Finally I could not pay the rent, was dispossessed, and then went to live in "Hell's Kitchen," in Thirty-ninth Street, where my son was born. Our friends thought the baby would bring Mary and me closer together, as it sometimes does. But what did I care for a baby!

I got work on Jake Sharp's Twenty-third Street cars, and Mary would bring me my dinner and do everything she could for me. But when drink is the idol—and it was mine—what does one care for love? Nothing. I certainly led Mary a hard life. At last I came home one night and she and the kid were gone. The baby was then two months old, and I never saw him again until he was a boy of nine. I was not sorry at their going. I wasn't any good in those days. I imagined I was "done dirty," as they say, but I knew the girl couldn't do anything else for herself and baby. I sold out the little furniture the rooms contained, got a few dollars, and jumped the town.

WANDERINGS

I started out with every one's hand against me and mine against every one's. I struck Marathon, N. Y., and had quite a time there. I worked in Dumphy's tannery, got a few weeks' pay and a few other articles, and jumped out for fear of being arrested. I reached Syracuse and struck a job in McChesney's lumberyard, at $1.35 per day.

I stayed in Syracuse quite a while and learned a little of the lumber business. I had quite a few adventures while there. I had struck up an acquaintance with a New York boy, and one evening after work we were sitting on the grass in front of one of the hotels, and seeing the patrol wagon passing, I made the remark, "Some poor bum is going to get a ride," when it pulled up in front of us and we were told to get in. I tried to argue the point with the captain, but it was of no use. We were taken to the station, and the others were sent below while I was kept up for examination. They put me through a light "third degree," measuring me and noting the color of hair and eyes, size of feet, etc.

Finally they stopped measuring and asking questions, and I waited. I saw my friend come up and go out of the door; he did not take time to bid me good-by. I asked the captain if he was through with me, and he did not know what to say. He apologized, and explained that I had been arrested because I looked like a man that had escaped from Auburn.

I felt rather sorry for the captain, not because I was not the escaped prisoner, but because he was so nervous. I could not leave him without a jolly, so I said, "Captain, if you'll come up to the corner I'll treat," patting my pocket in which I had a few pennies. He thanked me and said, "No." I met the captain every night taking his men as far as Salina Street, and we always saluted one another.

My new pal couldn't be got up on Main Street to the postoffice again for anything, and as soon as he earned money enough he took the train for "little old New York." I've met him on the Bowery since I became a missionary there, and we did smile about that ride in the "hurry-up wagon" in Syracuse.

Finally I came back to New York, after being away quite a time, got work in a carpet factory, and was quite steady for a while.

My poor dear mother was sick, sometimes up and oftentimes in bed. I can still see her and hear her say, "David, my poor boy, I do wish you would stop your drinking. I've prayed for you, and will pray until I die. Oh, Dave! I'd die so happy if my only son would stop and be a man!" But that cursed appetite, what a hold it had on me! It seemed as if I couldn't stop if I had been given all the money in the world.

I did love my mother dearly; I didn't care for any one in the world but her. Still, one of the meanest acts I ever did was to my mother. And such a good mother she was; there are not many like her!

She was in bed and had only a few weeks to live. One day she called me to her bedside and said, "Dave, I am going to leave you, never to see you again on this earth, but oh! how I wish you were going to meet me on the other side. Now, Dave, won't you promise me you will?" I said, "Yes, mother, sure I will." And she made me promise then and there that when she was dead, and waiting burial, I would not get drunk, at least while her body was in the house. I went down on my knees and promised her that I'd meet her in heaven.

She died, and the undertaker had been gone but a short time when I began drinking, and the day of the funeral I was pretty drunk. That was one of the meanest things I ever did. But I am sure that sometimes my dear mother looks over the portals of heaven, and sees her boy—a man now, a Christian—and forgives me. And some day, when my time comes, I am going to join her there.

I went from bad to worse, wandering all over, not caring what happened. I took a great many chances. Sometimes I had plenty of money, and at other times I wouldn't have a nickel I could jingle against a tombstone. I boated on the Ohio and Mississippi to New Orleans, then up on the Lakes. I was always wandering, but never at rest, sometimes in prison, and sometimes miles away from human habitation, often remorseful, always wondering what the end would be.

I recollect, after being eighty-two days on the river to New Orleans, being paid off with over $125. I left the steamer at Pittsburg, and the first thing I did was to go and get a jug of beer. Before I got anywhere near drunk I was before Judge White, and was fined $8.40, and discharged. I wasn't free half an hour before I was arrested again, brought before Judge White, and again fined $8.40. After being free for about fifteen minutes, I was again brought before Judge White, who looked at me this time and said, "Can't you keep sober?" I said, "Your Honor, I haven't had a drink since the first time." And I hadn't. But he said, "Five days," and I was shut up for that time, and I was in hell there five days if ever a man was.

Out of jail, I drifted with the tide. I was arrested for a trick that, if I had got my just dues, would have put me in prison for ten years, but I got off with three years, and came out after doing two years and nine months.

When a person is cooped up he has lots of time to think. It's think, think, think, and hope. Many's the time I said, "Oh, if I only get out and still have my health, what a change there will be!" And I meant it.

Isn't it queer how people will say, "I can't stop drinking," but when they're in jail they have to! The prison is a sanitarium for drunkards. They don't drink while on a visit there. Then why not stop it while one has a free foot? I thought of all these things while I was locked up, and I decided that when I was free I would hunt up my wife and baby and be a man.

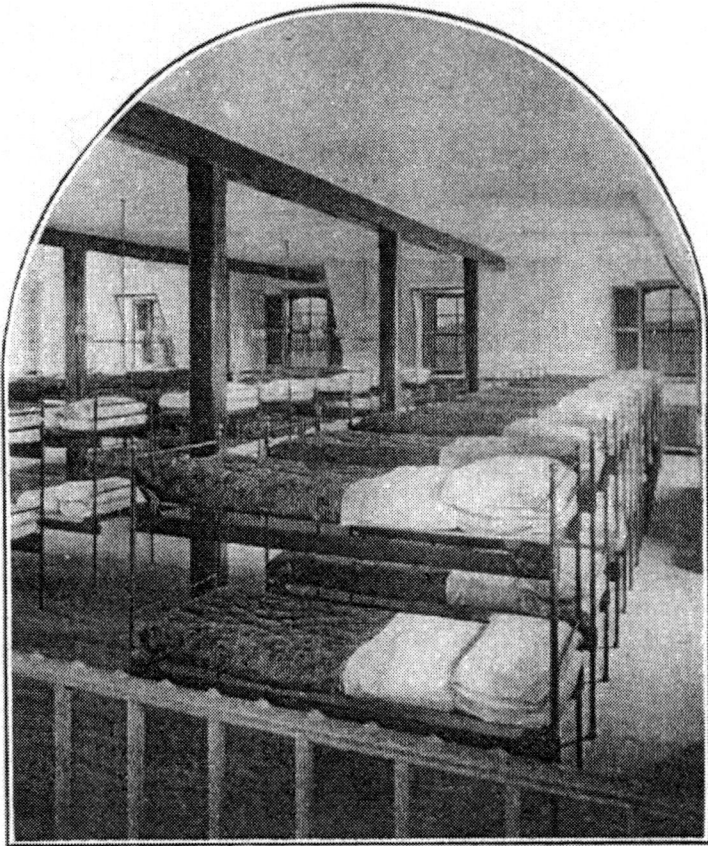

A BOWERY LODGING-HOUSE.

Prison at best isn't a pleasant place, but you can get the best in it if you behave. There's no coaxing you to be good. They won't say, "If you don't behave I'll send you home." It isn't like school. You have to behave or it's worse for you, for they certainly put you through some pretty tough things. Many's the time I got on my knees and told God all about it. If a man is crossing the street, sees a car coming, and is sure it will hit him, the first thing he says is, "Oh, God, save me!" The car misses him by a foot, and he forgets how much he owes. He simply says, "Thank you, God; when I'm in danger I'll call on You again." It was so with me. Out in the world again, I forgot all about all the promises I made in prison.

CHAPTER IV

"SAVED BY GRACE"

Twelve years later, after a life spent on the road and in prison, I found myself on the Bowery, in the fall of 1892, without a friend, "down and out." After spending my last dollar in — —'s saloon, I was sitting down in the back room of that place, wondering if I dared ask — — for a drink, when in he walked. He looked at me, and said, "Now, Danny, I think you had better get a move on! Get out and hustle. You are broke, and you know I am not running this place for fun."

I took it kind of hard, but looked at him and said, "All right." I got up from the chair where I'd been sitting and walked out, not caring what I did, but bound to get some money. Now, — — was a good fellow in his way; they all are if you have the price; but saloon-keepers are not running their places for the benefit of others, and when a man's money's gone they don't want him around. I had spent all I had, about twenty dollars, and now I was turned out, and it served me right.

Now there's something in rum that fascinates, something we can't understand. I wanted whiskey, and was ready to do anything to get it. The appetite in me was fierce. No one knows the terrible pangs, the great longing, but one who has been up against it. And nothing can satisfy the awful craving but whiskey.

THE TURNING-POINT

Many's the time I've stood on the Bowery and cursed God and the day I was born, and wished that I was dead. But here I was! Nobody cared for me, and why should they, for I did not care for myself. I did not even think God cared much or He would have done something. I imagined the Devil thought he had me for keeps, and so he did not exert himself very much either. I was out of the saloon, on the street, and little as I imagined such a thing would ever happen, I never entered — —'s saloon again. All unknown to me the turning-point in my life had come.

Sizing up the situation, I knew I must have a drink, but how was I to get it? Up to this time I'd done everything on the calendar except murder, and I don't know how I missed that. I've seen men killed, have been in a few shoot-ups myself, and bear some scars, but I know at this writing that God and a mother's prayers saved me from this awful crime.

Among the many accomplishments suited to the life I was leading was that of a "strong-arm man," and I determined to put it into use now, for I was desperate.

The rule in this dastardly work is always to select a man smaller and weaker than one's self. As I looked about I saw a man coming up the Bowery who seemed to answer to the requirements, and I said to myself, "This is my man!" I walked up to him and touched him on the shoulder, but as he straightened up I saw that he was as big as myself, and I hesitated. I would have taken the chances even then, but he started back and asked what I wanted. I said I was hungry, thinking that he would put his hand in his pocket, and then, having only one hand, I could put the "strangle hold" on him. But he was equal to the situation. He told me afterward that I looked dangerous.

I asked him if he was ever hungry. He said, "Many's the time." I told him I was starving. "Come with me," said he, and we went over to Chatham Square, to a place called "Beefsteak John's."

We went in and sat down, and he said, "Now order what you want." On the Bowery in those days you could get a pretty good meal for fifteen cents—all you wanted to eat. The waiter was there to take my order. I knew him and winked to him to go away, and he went. He thought I was going to work the young fellow for his money.

The young fellow said, "Why don't you call for something? I thought you were starving."

Now here I was up against it. I'd panned this man for something to eat, and he was willing to pay for anything I wanted, and for the life of me I could not swallow any food. When a man is drinking he doesn't care to eat at a table. Give him a square meal, and he doesn't enjoy it. I know men to-day who spend every dollar they earn for drink, and eat nothing but free lunches, handed out with their drinks. That was what was the matter with me. All I wanted was drink. The young man had called my bluff, and I had nothing to show but lies. I sat there wondering how I was going to get out of this hole. I was looking at the man and he at me, when the little good that was in me cropped out, and looking him square in the eye I said, "Young fellow, I've lied to you. I could not eat the first mouthful." I told him I'd gone up to him thinking he would dig down in his pocket and give me a little change. I did not mention the fact that I intended to "put him up in the air" and rob him. Then I sat back in my chair and waited for the "come-back." Finally he said, "Have some coffee and sinkers"—rolls. But I could not go even that!

We got to talking, and he asked me where I was living. I smiled at the idea of my living! I wasn't even existing! I told him I lived any place where I hung up my hat: that I didn't put up at the Astor House very often; sometimes at the Delevan, or the Windsor, or in fact, any of the hotels on the Bowery were good enough for me—that is, if I had the price, fifteen cents. You can get a bed in a lodging-house for ten cents, or if you have only seven cents you can get a "flop." You can sit in some joint all night if you have a nickel, but if you haven't you can do the next best thing in line, and that is "carry the banner." Think of walking the streets all night and being obliged to keep moving!

The man took a fifty-cent piece out of his pocket, held it in his hand, and asked me if I would meet him at the Broome Street Tabernacle the next morning at ten-thirty. Now I wanted that half-dollar, I wanted it badly! It meant ten drinks to me at five per. I would have promised to meet the Devil in hell for drink, and fearing the young man might put the money in his pocket again, I said I'd be there. He gave me the half-dollar, we shook hands, and I never expected to see that man again.

I didn't go back to — —'s, but to — — Bowery—another place that has put more men on the down-grade than any place I know. It's out of business now, and as I pass there every day I pray that all the saloons may go. I drank the half-dollar up in quick time, for with the Bowery element it's divy even with drinks.

BROOME STREET TABERNACLE

Morning came, and I wondered what I should do for the day. How I loved to stand and smell the liquor, even when not drinking! But now I hate it! Oh, what a change when Christ comes into a man's heart! I had stood there all night in that saloon and didn't feel a bit tired. I went out to "do" some one else, when I thought of the fellow of last night. I thought I had sized him up and that he was easy, so I started for the meeting-place, the Tabernacle. I went there to see if I could work him for a dollar, or perhaps two.

I got to the church and looked for a side door and found a bell which I rang. I did not have to wait long before the young fellow himself opened the door. Out went his hand, and he gave me such a shake that one would have thought he had known me all my life. There's a lot in a handshake! "I'm glad to see you!" he said. "I knew you would keep your promise. I knew you would come."

That took me back a little. Here was a man I had never seen till the night before taking me at my word. I wondered who he was. We went into the church. He was talking to make me feel at home. Finally he looked me over from head to feet and said, "Are those the best clothes you have?" I said, "These are the best and only clothes I have." I had my trunk on my back, and the whole kit, shoes and all, wasn't worth fifty cents. The way of the drunkard is hard. I had helped put diamonds on the saloon-keeper and rags on myself, but if there are any diamonds now I'll put them on my own little wife and not the saloon-keeper's. The young man said, "I've a nice suit that will fit you. Will you let me give it to you?"

Here was a situation that puzzled me. I was an old offender, had "been up" many times and was well known to the police. My record was bad, and whenever there was a robbery or hold-up the police would round up all the ex-convicts and line us up at headquarters for identification. Give a dog a bad name and it sticks. I was suspicious; a man that has "done time" always is; and when the young man said he had clothes for me, I put him down as one of the "stool pigeons" working in with the police. Since I'd graduated to the Bowery doing crooked work I imagined every one was against me. It was a case of "doing" others or they would "do" me. And I wondered why this man took such an interest in me. The more I thought the more puzzled I got.

I looked about me. I was in a church; why should he do me any harm? Then I thought that if I put on the clothes he might slip an Ingersoll watch into the pocket, let me get on the street, and then shout "Stop, thief!" I'd be arrested and then it would be away up the river for a good long bit. However, I'm a pretty good judge of human nature, and I thought I'd take a chance. It was a fine suit; and I could just see myself putting it in pawn, so I said I'd take it. But "there's many a slip 'twixt the cup and lip," and there was a strange slip in my case.

The young fellow said, "Don't you think you had better have a bath?" Well, I did need a bath for fair. A man sleeping in one bed one night and a different one the next, walking the streets and sitting around on park benches, gets things on him, and they are grandparents in a couple of nights. Of course I needed a bath! I was a walking menagerie! He gave me some money, and I went out and had a bath and came back with the change. He showed me where I could change my clothes, and there was a whole outfit laid out for me, underwear and all.

I thought the man was crazy. I could not understand. At last I got into the clothes, and I felt fine. I got a look at myself in the glass, and I looked like a full-fledged Bowery politician. I said as I looked, "Is this me or some other fellow?" I weighed one hundred and ninety pounds and was five feet ten inches tall.

I went into the young man's study and sat down. I did not know what was coming next, perhaps money. I was ready for anything, for I took him for a millionaire's son.

Up to this time he had said nothing to me about God. Finally he opened up and asked my name. I told him Dave Ranney, but I had a few others to use in a pinch. And I told him the truth; kindness had won.

He said, "Dave, why are you leading such a life? Don't you know you were cut out for a far better one?" I was no fool; I knew all about that. I had learned it in Sunday-school, and how often mother had told me the same thing. I knew I was put into the world to get the best, and glorify God; and I was getting the worst, and it was all my own fault. Here I was. I felt that no one wanted anything to do with me, no one would trust me, because I was a jail-bird. But I have found out since there are people that are willing to help a man if they see he is on the level.

"Why," I said, "a man that has no backing has no show in 'little old New York.' You even have to have a pull to get a job shoveling snow, and then you have to buy your own shovel! What does any one care? The politicians have all they want and are only looking for more graft. They need you just twice a year to register and vote. I know I'm crooked, and it's my own fault, I admit, but who's going to give me a chance? Oh, for a chance!"

The young fellow listened, then said, "Dave, there's One that will help."

I did not catch on to his meaning, but said I was glad and thanked him for what he had done. I thought he meant himself. "Not I," he said; "I mean God. Why don't you give Him a chance? Talk about men giving you a chance—why, God is waiting for a chance to help you!"

Just then my old friend the Devil came in; he always does when he thinks he is going to lose a convert; and he said in his own fine way, "Oh, what rot! Why didn't God help you before this? Don't bother about it; you have a nice suit; get out of this place and sell the duds and have a good time. I'll help you. I'll be your friend." He's sly, but I put him behind me that time.

It was easy enough for this man to talk about God giving me a chance, but he didn't know me—a hard, wicked sinner, who if half the crimes I had committed were known I'd be put in prison for life. Would God help such a one? I knew I was clean and had a good suit of clothes on, but, oh! how I wished God would give me another chance! But I felt as if He had no use for me.

The man put his hand on my shoulder and said, "I want to be your friend; will you let me?" I said I'd be proud of such a friend. "Now, Dave," he said, "there's One better than I who will stick to you closer than a brother; will you let Him be your friend?" I said I would, though I doubted if He wanted any part of me, but I was going to make a try; and the young man and myself knelt down in the Tabernacle, corner of Broome Street and Centre Market Place, on the 16th of September, 1892, and I asked God to have mercy on me, cut the drink out of my life, and make a man of me, if such a thing could be done, for Christ's sake. I kept praying that over and over again, the man still kneeling with me, when all of a sudden I heard a voice say, "I will, Dave; only trust Me and have faith." I heard those words just as sure as I am living, and writing this book. None but a Christian can understand this voice; others would say we are crazy who say such things; but it's true: only have faith, and all things are yours. I've proved it!

A NEW MAN IN CHRIST JESUS

I rose from my knees a changed man. I can't explain it, but I felt as I hadn't felt in years—lighter, happier, with a peace that was great in my heart. I thought of mother and only wished she could see me then, but she did all right.

"What will your friends say?" there was the old Devil saying. "Get out of this place, and don't be a fool; be a man."

I stood there listening to the tempter, when the young fellow said, "Dave, what are you going to do now that you have taken Jesus?"

I said, "I've knelt here and asked God for Christ's sake to make me a sober man, and I fully believe that He will. Drink has brought me down, and I'll die before I'll take another drink." And at this writing I'm over seventeen years off the stuff.

I asked the young fellow what his name was, and found that he was Alexander Irvine, lodging-house missionary to the Bowery under the New York City Mission of which Dr. Schauffler is the head. We shook hands, and before we parted we made a compact that we would be pals.

Isn't it wonderful what God can do? I don't believe there's a man or woman, no matter how wicked, no matter what sin they've done, but God can and will save, the only conditions being: Come, believe, and trust. "For God so loved the world that He gave His only-begotten Son, that whosoever believeth in Him should not perish, but have everlasting life." —John 3:16. But you have to have some sand of your own.

READING-ROOM IN A LODGING-HOUSE.

CHAPTER V

ON THE UP GRADE

Mr. Irvine paid for my lodging and meals for a week at 105 Bowery. I thought he was great; I'd never run up against anything like him. He said, "We must get you a job of some kind, and that quick. Will you work?" Well, what do you think of that! Would I work? It struck me as funny. Work and I had fallen out long ago. I could lie down beside work and watch the other fellow do it. I had reached the point where, like a good many others, I felt the world owed me a living, and I was bound to get it. I had toiled hard and faithfully for the Devil, and taken a great many chances, and I never thought of that as work. And I got the wages the Devil always pays—cuts, shot, prison: I was paid good and plenty. Here I was up against another proposition—work—and I hated it!

Irvine said, "You must have something to occupy your mind and time, for you know the Devil finds mischief for idlers." I said I'd tackle anything; I'd work all right. A few days later he told me he had a job for me. "Good," I said. I wondered what kind of work it was. I knew it was not a position of great trust, not a cashier in a bank; that would have to come later on. Well, the job was tending a furnace—get up steam at 5 A. M., do the chores, and make myself generally useful; wages $12.00 per month and my breakfast!

I did not like this for a starter, and I told Mr. Irvine so, and he had to do some tall talking. He finally got angry and said, "Ranney, you started out to let God help you. Well, you know God helps the man that helps himself." That was so. I had asked God to help me, and here I was at the start refusing to give Him a chance. That clinched it, and I took the first honest job I had had in a good many years. I thank God I did take it, for it was a stepping-stone.

FISHING FOR A DINNER

I started in working and was getting on fine, but I always felt I wasn't getting money enough. I tried in my leisure time for another job, but in all the places I was asked the same question: "Where did you work last?" I could not tell them, "In prison and on the road," and that queered me. So I stuck to the furnace, was always on time, and was pretty well liked by the people. I had been there about two weeks, and seen the cook every day and smelled the steak, etc., about noontime and at supper, but the cook never asked me if I had a mouth on me. She was a good-natured outspoken Irish woman with a good big heart, and I thought about this time that I'd jolly her a little and get my dinner. One day I came up from the cellar carrying a hod of coal in each hand, and going into the kitchen I tried in every way to attract her attention, but she was busy broiling a steak and never looked around. Finally I got tired and said, "Cook, where will I put this coal?" Well, well, I'll never forget that moment in years! She turned and looked at me and began, "I want you to understand my name is Mrs. Cunningham. I'm none of your cooks, and if you dare call me cook again while you're in this house I'll have you sacked—discharged!" I thought I had been hit with a steam car. I did not answer her back, and she kept right on: "I'm a lady, and I'll be treated as such or I'll know why!" I never saw a person so mad in all my life, and I couldn't understand why. There she was cooking, and yet she was no cook! I thought to myself, "I guess she doesn't like her job." I didn't blame her, because I didn't like mine either.

My heart went down into my boots. Here I had made a play for a dinner and got left. About a week after this I was doing a little job in the laundry when I ran across the cook, and she said, "Young man, would you like a little bite to eat?" I answered quickly, "Yes, thank you, Mrs. Cunningham," just as sweet as anything. No more "cook" for mine. I'll never call people by their occupation again as long as I live. I'd had my lesson; but I had won out on my dinner too. A short time after she asked me if I could read, and would I read the news to her while she was peeling potatoes. I answered very sweetly, "Yes, Mrs. Cunningham," and I got my supper.

I would see Irvine once in a while, and I was always ready to give up my job, but he would say, "Stay six months, get a recommend, and then you can get something better. Just let God take care of you, and you'll come out away on top of the heap. God is going to use you in His work. Just keep on trusting and don't get discouraged." He always had a word of cheer, and I thank God that I did trust, and things came out better than I even thought.

You readers who are just starting out in the Christian life, just let God have His way. Don't think you know it all. Go right ahead, have a little sand, and trust Him. He will never leave you, and you will have the best in this life and in the life to come. It's an everlasting joy, and isn't it worth working for, boys?

PRAYERS IN A LODGING-HOUSE

I remember, when I knelt down in 105 Bowery beside my cot to ask God's blessing and guidance, how a laugh used to go around the dormitory. There were about seventy beds in the place, and it was something unusual to see a man on his knees praying. But when I started out to be a man I meant business, and I said I would say my prayers every night. I don't think God can think much of a man who says his prayers lying on his back, unless he's sick. I believe God expects us to get on our knees, for if a thing is worth getting it's worth thanks. I didn't mind the laugh so much, but I did some: it was sort of cutting. I'm no coward physically, and can handle myself fairly well at the present time, but when it came to getting on my knees I was a rank coward.

A lodging-house is a queer affair. Men of all nations sleep there—some drunk, some dreaming aloud, others snoring. The cots are about two feet apart—just room for you to pass between them. It takes a lot of grit and plenty of God's grace to live a Christian life in a lodging-house. I go in them every day now to look after the other fellow: if he is sick or wants to go to the hospital I'll see to that; but I never can forget the time when I was one of those, inmates.

One night I had just got on my knees when boots, shoes, and pillows came sailing at me; one boot hit me, and it did hurt for fair. Then a whiskey flask hit me, and that hurt. I was boiling with rage. I got up, but I didn't say anything; no one would have answered me if I had; they were all asleep, by the way. We call such business hazing, but it's mean and dirty.

I went to work as usual the next day, and thought and planned all day how to catch one of those fellows. I figured out the following plan: I did not go to bed that night until quite late; the gas was turned down low, and I made noise enough for them to hear me. When I was ready for bed I knelt down and turned my head as quick as a flash to catch the throwers, for I knew they would throw again. Just as I turned I caught the fellow in the act of throwing a bottle. It seemed as though the Devil had got me for fair again, for I made a rush for that fellow, got him by the throat, pulled him out of bed and jumped on him, and I think if it hadn't been for the watchman I would have killed him; but he said, "Dan, for God's sake don't kill him!" I let up, and, standing upon that dormitory floor, beds all around, every one awake, about 11 P. M., I gave my first testimony, which was something like this: "Men, I've quit drinking—been off the stuff about two weeks, a thing I have not done in years unless locked up. I've knelt and asked God to keep me sober and have thanked Him for His kindness to me. Now if you men don't let me alone in the future I'll lick you or you will me."

I went to my cot and knelt down, but I was so stirred up I couldn't pray. I wondered if there was going to be any more throwing, but that night finished it. I went up in the opinion of those men one hundred per cent. I lived there until the place burned down, and was one of the fortunate ones that got out alive when so many lost their lives, and I always said my prayers and was respected by the men. I was making lots of friends and attending Sunday-school, prayer-meeting, and mission services.

THE STORY OF AN OVERCOAT

One Thanksgiving-time I was hired to carry dinners to the poor families by the New York City Mission. Mrs. Lucy Bainbridge was the superintendent. God bless her, for she was and is one good woman! I didn't have any overcoat and it was cold; but I didn't mind, as I was moving about carrying the dinners. This was about two months after I had decided to follow Christ, and I still had the furnace job when I met Mrs. Bainbridge.

She knew me by sight and asked me how I was getting on, and where was my overcoat? I told her I was getting along all right, but I had no overcoat. She said, "That's too bad! Come with me and we will see if there's one in the Dorcas Room" —a place where clothes are kept that good people send in for the poor who haven't so much. There were quite a few coats there, any one of which would have suited me, but they didn't please Mrs. Bainbridge. She said, "David, come into the office." She gave me a letter to Rogers, Peet & Co., and told me to take it down there and wait for an answer.

I went down and gave the letter to a clerk, and it was great to see him eye me up. I didn't know then how the letter read, but have since learned that the contents were as follows: "Give this man about the best overcoat you have in the store." No wonder he looked me over!

We began trying on coats, found one that suited us, and he said, "You might as well wear it home." "Not on your natural!" I said. "Put it in paper or a box." I didn't think that coat was for me, for it was fifty dollars if a cent. Picture me with twelve dollars per month and three meals, and a fifty-dollar overcoat!

I went back to Mrs. Bainbridge, and she told me to try the coat on, which I did. Then she said, "David, that coat is for you, but listen, David; that coat is mine. Now I wouldn't go into a saloon, and I want you to promise me that you will never enter a saloon while you wear it." I promised, and that coat never went into a saloon, and I wore it for five years. Then I sent it to old Ireland, to my wife's father, and perhaps he is still wearing it. I often see Mrs. Bainbridge, and she is always the same kind friend, God bless her! I have entry to the Dorcas Room when I need anything to help a man that I'm trying to put on his feet, and that's often.

DELIVERING TELEPHONE BOOKS

It was coming spring and I was no longer needed at the furnace. I left with a recommendation for six months and a standing invitation from the cook for my meals, and she never went back on me. I don't know where she is now, but if she reads this book I want her to know that I appreciated all she did for me when I started this new life and I am sure she will be delighted to know that she helped a little.

I got another job delivering telephone books. When you see a poor seedy-looking man delivering these books, give him a kind word, for there's many a good man at that job to-day hoping for something better. This job was a hard one and you had to hustle to make a dollar a day, but I did not mind the hustling: I was strong, the drink had gone out of me, and I felt good. I was anxious to get a job as porter in some wholesale house, and delivering these books gave me a good chance to ask, and ask I did in nearly every store where I delivered a book. I always got the same reply, "No one wanted." I stayed at this about three months, and was getting discouraged. It looked as though I'd never get a steady position.

I had only a few more days of work, and was just finishing my deliveries one afternoon. I had Twenty-second Street and North River as my last delivery, which took me into the lumber district and into the office of John McC— —. I asked the young man in charge of the office if they wanted a young fellow to work. He asked me what I could do, and I said, "Anything." Now it's an old saying, "A man that can do everything can't do much of anything."

We went down into the yard and he asked me the different qualities of lumber and their names. I'll never forget the first question he asked me, which was, "What's the name of that piece of timber?" I said, "Oak," and I was right. After testing me on the other piles he asked me if I could measure, and could I tally? I told him I could, and he said, "I'll give you $9.00. Is that enough?" I said that would do for a starter, and he told me to be on hand at seven o'clock in the morning.

41

I delivered the few books I had left, drew my money, got a shave, bought a leather apron, and went to bed. I was up and at John McC— —'s yard at 6:30.

He was Police Commissioner then, and one of the whitest men I ever ran up against.

I started in at my third job since I had been converted. I was at home in the lumber yard, as I had learned the business While roughing it in Tonawanda, Troy, Syracuse, Buffalo, and on the Lakes. And when a man learns anything, if he isn't a fool he can always work at it again. Here I was at a business few could tell me much about.

MR. RANNEY AND ONE OF HIS "BOYS."

TESTIFYING IN A LUMBER YARD

The lumber-handlers as a rule are a free and easy set, nearly all drinking men. It's warm work, and when a man is piling all day, pulling up plank after plank, he thinks a pint of beer does him good. They rush the can—first the piler, then the stager, and then the ground man, then the piler again, and so on. I've counted as many as twenty pints in one day among one gang. I soon got the run of the yard and made friends with all the men; but if ever I was up against temptation it was there in that yard, where I worked a long time. They would ask me to have a drink, but I told them time and time again that I did not care about it; I was off the stuff.

Often when I was sweating after pushing down a load of lumber from the pile and keeping tally at the same time, the Devil would whisper to me, "Oh, have a glass of beer; it won't hurt you; it will do you good," and I was tempted to join with the men and drink. I had to keep praying hard and fast, for I was sorely tempted. But, thank God, I've yet to take my first drink since 1892!

God was always near me, and He often said, "Tell the men all about it, how you have asked Me to help you, and they won't ask you to drink any more." I wondered what the men would say if I told them. I was a little timid about doing it. I had testified once or twice in a meeting, but that was easy compared with this. But after a while I got up courage and told the men why I did not drink. I said, "I have been a hard man and loved drink so much that it separated me from family and friends, put me in prison, and took my manhood away. One year ago I took Jesus as my helper and asked Him to take away this love for drink, and He did. I would rather lose my right arm than go back again, and with God's help I'll win out and never drink again." I often talked with them about it, told them it was a good way to live, and to think it over. I found out in a little while that the men thought better of me, and respected me more than before. I have heard some of them say, "I wish I could give up the drink," and some did, and are living good lives without the cursed stuff.

I've met some of these men on the Bowery, "down and out," and I've stood by them and tried to point them in the right direction. There's one man, a fine noble fellow, who used to work with me in my lumber days, who is on the Bowery at the present time, unable to give up the drink. He is always glad to see me and says, "God bless you, Dan, and keep you away from the stuff. I wish I could!" I tell him to ask God and have faith, and then I slip him a meal ticket and give him a God bless you!

DAVE RANNEY, ALIAS DANNY REILLY.

CHAPTER VI

PROMOTED

I had never lost sight of my friend Irvine. We used to see each other often and have a good chat about things in general. He said he was going to take charge of the Sea and Land Church and wanted me to come and be the sexton. It would give me $30.00 per month, rooms, coal and gas. He thought it would be a good thing for me to become reunited to my wife Mary, and I thought so too, but she had to give her consent. We had been separated for a number of years, and though I had been calling on her for over a year she never took any stock in my conversion. Here I was fifteen months a redeemed man, trying to get my wife to live with me again. I prayed often, but I never thought she would consent.

CHURCH OF SEA AND LAND

I was married young, and she was only a girl, and though she loved me she could not forget the misery and hardships she went through. I never hit her in my life, but I wouldn't support her: I'd rather support the rumseller and his family, all for that cursed drink. And I didn't blame her for being afraid to chance it again. "A burnt child dreads the fire." I had made her life very hard, and she was afraid. She was glad to know that I had given up drink, but doubted my remaining sober. Finally she agreed to live with me again if I remained sober for three years. I was put on probation—the Methodist way. Now I had been on the level for fifteen months, and I had twenty-one months more to go. She was strong-minded and would stick to her word, so I did not see how I could take the job as sexton.

I told Mr. Irvine that was the way things stood and for him to get some one else. He said, "Pretty slim chances, but we will pray about it." He and I went up to Sixty-seventh Street, where Mrs. Ranney

45

was working as laundress, and after a little talk we came to the point. I was a go-ahead man, and tried every way to get her to promise to come down, but she wouldn't say yes. I'll never forget that night in the laundry if I live a hundred years; she took no stock in me at all. I was giving it up as a bad job; she wouldn't come, and that settled it. We got up to go when Mr. Irvine asked if she would object to a word of prayer. She said, "No," and we had a little prayer-meeting right there. We bade Mrs. Ranney good-night and left.

The next night she came down and we showed her all over the church. The sexton who had been living there hadn't kept the living apartments clean, and she did not like them very much, but when she went away she said, "If I only could be sure you would keep sober I would go with you, but I can't depend on you. Fifteen months isn't long enough; you will have to go three years. I don't think I'll come." I said, "That settles it! But listen: whether you come or not, I am not going back to the old life." The next day I received a telegram from Mary saying,

"COME UP FOR MY THINGS."

I jumped on a single truck, drove up to Sixty-seventh Street, and got all my wife's things, trunks, band-boxes and everything, and it did not take me long to get down to the church. Mary was already there, and I took charge of the Church of the Sea and Land at Market and Henry Streets, where I remained as sexton for ten years. I would not take $10,000 for the character I received from the trustees when I resigned. I always look back with pleasure to those good old days at the church, the many friends we made, and the many blessings I received while there.

It did not take us long to get the run of the place. We sent for our boy, who was in Ireland with his mother's folks. When he came I didn't know him, as I hadn't seen him since he was a little baby. What a surprise it was when at my sister's house, after supper, she went into the front room, leaving me alone in the kitchen, when a manly little fellow came in and looked me over and said, "Hello, father, I'm your son Willie. How are you?"

I looked at him, but couldn't say a word, for I had almost forgotten that I had a son. I opened my arms and the boy came with a rush, threw his arms around my neck, and said, "I love you, dad."

I want to say here that this boy has never given me any trouble and we have been companions ever since that night. He married a good Christian girl and is in his own home to-day.

I heard a little laugh, and there were my sister and Mary taking it all in. I could see then that it was a put-up job, this getting me to go up to my sister's house.

Time passed and we were doing finely. One day we heard the boy playing the piano, and we got him a teacher. In a short time he was able to play for the smaller classes, the juniors. Then my friend Mrs. Bainbridge got him a better teacher. He improved rapidly, and now he is organist in the Fifty-seventh Street Presbyterian Church.

I tell you it pays to be a Christian and on the level. If I hadn't done anything else but give that boy a musical education, it would have paid. I'm proud of him.

MY FIRST SERMON

I remember the first meeting I ever led. It came about like this: I had been sexton of Sea and Land Church about four years, was growing in grace and getting on finely. One Wednesday night the minister asked me if I would lead the prayer-meeting the following week, as he was going away. I told him I did not know how to lead a meeting and I was afraid to undertake it, as I couldn't preach a sermon. "Oh, that's all right," he said. "I'll write out something, and all you will have to do is to study it a little, read it over once or twice, then get up and read it off." I told him I'd try. I'd do the best I could. So he wrote about ten sheets of foolscap paper, all about sinners. I remember there was a story about a man going over the falls in a boat, and lots of other interesting things as I thought. I took the paper home and studied as hard as I could to get it into my head.

The night came on which I was to take the meeting—that eventful night in my life. I got on the platform, took the papers out of my pocket, and opened the big Bible at the chapter I was going to read, and laid out the talk just as I thought a minister might do. I read the chapter, then we had a song, then it was up to me.

Do you know I made the greatest mistake of my life that night! I went on that platform trusting in my own strength and not asking God's help. I got a swelled head and imagined I was the real thing. But God in His own way showed me where I was standing and brought me up with a short turn.

I began reading the article written, and was getting on well, as I thought, taking all the credit myself and not giving God any. I read three pages all right, when some one opened the window. It was a March night, very windy, and when the window was opened something happened, and I thank God that it did.

The wind came directly toward me and took the sermon I was preaching and scattered it all over the room. I didn't know what to say or do. I forgot everything that was written on the papers, and I knew if I tried to get them back I would make a fool of myself.

There was a smile on every face in the congregation. There I stood, wishing the floor would open and let me through. I certainly was in a box!

Just at this moment God spoke to me and said, "David, I did that, and I did it for your own good. Now listen to me. You were not cut out for a minister. Just get up and tell these people how God for Christ's sake saved you, and I'll be with you."

I listened to the voice, bowed my head in prayer, and it seemed as though the Lord put the words in my mouth. I told that roomful of people of my past life and how God saved and had blessed me for four years. We had a grand meeting and a number were saved that night, and, above all, I received one of the greatest blessings of my life.

On his return the minister said, "I hear you had a great meeting. How did the reading go!" I told him what had happened, and he was astonished, but saw God's hand in it, and said so.

From that night on I never wrote up anything to read to my audience, and I have spoken all over within a circle of fifty miles of New York, and even farther away, including Boston, Philadelphia, Albany, and Troy. I tell the Bowery boys I'm what is called an extemporaneous talker. I don't know the first word I'm going to say when I get on my feet, but God never leaves me: I just open my mouth and He fills it. Praise His name!

It was a lesson to me and I have never forgotten it.

THE TESTIMONY OF A GAMBLER

While I was sexton of the old Sea and Land Church I met among other men one who came to be a great friend. We called ourselves pals and loved each other dearly, and yet I have never been able to bring him to Christ. When I told him I was writing the story of my life he said he wanted to add a few lines to tell, he said, what I could not. This is what he wrote:

"'Lead, Kindly Light,' was the song; I'll never forget it. I heard it on the Bowery fifteen years ago. I was passing a Mission, and hearing it I went in—I don't know why to this day. After the singing some one prayed, and I started to go out when the leader of the meeting called for testimonies for Christ. I waited and listened, and I heard a voice that made me sit down again. I shall never forget the man that was speaking. What he said sounded like the truth. It was the greatest sermon I ever listened to. He was telling how much God had done for him, saved him from drink and made a Christian man of him. I knew it was the truth. I went home that night to wife and children, and told my wife where I had been. She laughed and said, 'Dan, you are getting daffy.' From that night on I have been a better husband and father.

"I left home one night about six o'clock and went down Cherry Street to a saloon where the gang hang out. I had been telling the boys about the things I had heard at the Mission. A young man said, 'Sullivan, there was a young preacher down at my house and asked me to come to a young people's meeting at the Sea and Land Church. I promised I would go, but I haven't got the courage.' In a moment I got churchy. I had never been in a church in New York. I said, 'Come on,' and we went to that meeting. I am glad I did. That night I met my friend Ranney. As I was passing out of the meeting he greeted me—he was the sexton—with a handshake and a 'Good-night, old pal; come again!' There is something in a handshake, and as we shook I felt I had made another friend. I'll never forget that night. We became fast friends. There is no one that knows Ranney better than Sullivan. I have watched him in his climb to the top step by step to be in the grand position he fills, that of Lodging House Missionary to the Bowery under the New York City Mission and Tract Society.

"One day we were going up the Bowery and passing a Mission went in. We heard the testimonies, and I turned to Ranney and said, 'Are you a Christian?' He said, 'I am.' I said, 'Get up, then, and tell the men what God has done for you.' Now here I was a gambler telling this man to acknowledge God, and I did not do it myself! Ranney rose and turned all colors. He finally settled down to that style of talking which he alone possesses. He told his story for the first time. I have heard him hundreds of times since, but to me that night fifteen years ago was the greatest talk he ever gave, telling how God saved him from a crooked and drunken life. It had the ring! I loved him from that night on. When he got through I said, 'Dave, God met you face to face to-night. You will be a different man from now on. God spoke to-night, not you. It was the best talk I ever heard. It took you a long time to start, but nothing can stop you now. One word of advice, pal, I'll give you: Don't get stuck on yourself. God will use you when He won't others among your own kind. He will make a preacher of you to men of your own stamp.' And Ranney is to-day what I said and thought he would be.

"You would think that a man who had been the pal of Ranney for three years would never say an unkind word to one that he loved, but that is what I did. We had a misunderstanding, and I said things to Dave Ranney that he never will forget. I called him every name on the calendar. He was speechless and I thought afraid of me. He never said a word. I left him standing there as if petrified—his friend and pal talking to him like that, his pal that sang with him, and joked with him!

"I went home and swore that never again would I have anything to do with a Christian. I had forgotten for the moment all the little kindnesses he had done and how after I had been on a drunk he had been at my bedside, how he had spoken words of cheer and comfort and said, 'Dan, old man, cheer up. Some day you are going to cut out drink'; and I want to say right now that I have not drank in over twelve years. I'd forgotten all that. I only thought of how I might hang the best fellow on this earth. I came to myself ten minutes after I left him, but the work had been done, and I made up my mind I'd never see or speak to him again. I'd go back to my old life of gambling and cheating, and I did.

"Five months passed. I had not seen Ranney in all that time. I was playing poker one night, the 16th of September, 1899, with no more thought of Dave than if he had never lived. It was in the old — — — — Hotel on Water Street, a little before eight in the evening. My partner and I were having a pretty easy time stealing the other men's money—some call it cheating—when my thoughts turned to my old Christian pal Ranney. It was the eighth anniversary of his conversion. Quick as a flash I jumped to my feet and said, 'Boys, I'll be back in an hour. I've got to go!' My partner thought I had been caught cheating and was going to cash his chips. I said, 'I'll be back in a little while.'

"I ran all the way up to the Bowery to the place where Ranney was holding his meeting. The Mission was packed. There were a lot of big-guns on the platform. No one saw me that knew me. Ranney was asking for those testimonies that would help the other fellow. I got on my feet and faced him. He turned pale. He thought I was going to set him out then and there. He looked me straight in the eye and began to come slowly toward me, and when I had finished we had one another by the hand. This is part of what I said that night:

"'I make no pretense at being a Christian. I am a gambler. But the man standing there—Dave Ranney—was once my chum and pal. We had a little misunderstanding some five months ago, and I am here to-night to ask his forgiveness. Forgive me, Dave. I just left a card-game to come up to your anniversary and help make you happy. I know you don't believe I meant what I said. I love you more to-night than any time since I first met you. Why, men, I would lay down my life that Ranney is one of the best and whitest Christians in New York to-night. It ain't the big things that a man does that show his real character. No, it's the little things. I have watched Ranney, been with him; his sorrows are my sorrows, his joys my joys. I can't say any more to-night.'

"Dave begged me to stay. Mr. Seymour came down to speak to me, but I'd done what I came to do, and I had got out quick—from Heaven to Hell, from my Christian pal to my pal in crime at the card-table.

"I've never been converted. If I was I'd go like my pal Ranney out in the world and tell how God saved me, and not let the ministers do all the talking. At present all I can say is, 'God bless my pal! and some of these days perhaps I'll be with him on the platform telling what God did for me. God speed the day!'"

TRIED IN THE FIRE

I had been sexton for over five years, and had been greatly blessed, when my wife became ill. Things did not always run smoothly, for there are ups and downs even in a sexton's life, and I had mine. When Mary and I took up again I determined to do all in my power to make amends for my former treatment of her, to make life as pleasant for her as I could, and I did. When she was first taken sick I sent her and the boy over to Ireland to visit her parents, thinking the change would do her good. She was better for a little while, but on the 14th of March, 1902, she died. My boy and I were at her bedside and promised to meet her on the other side, and with the help of God we are going to keep our word.

You know there are always "knockers," and I knew quite a few. In every church and society there they are with their little hatchets ready to trim and knock any one that goes ahead of them. Some of these people said of me, "Oh, Ranney is under Christian influences. He is sexton. He is afraid. Wait until he runs up against a lot of trouble, then he will go back to the Bowery again and drink worse than ever." I do think some of those people would have liked to see it happen. I've seen one of them in a sanitarium to be treated for drink who was my worst knocker, and I told him I would pray for him. I'm not talking of the good Christian people. They don't know how to "knock," and I thank God for all such. I had a thousand friends for every "knocker," and they were ready to help me with kind words, money, or in any other way when I was in trouble.

Just as an illustration of this take the act of the poor fellows of the Midnight Mission in Chinatown when my wife died. They wanted to show their sympathy and their love, and a delegation of them came in a body and placed a wreath on Mary's coffin. I learned afterwards how they all chipped in for the collection—some a few cents, some a nickel. Don't think for a moment that the Bowery down-and-out has no heart, for it isn't so. Many a tough-looking fellow with a jumper instead of a shirt has one of the truest hearts that beats. I only wish I could help them more than I do.

When God took Mary away I thought it was hard, and I was sore and ready to do anything, I didn't care what. There was a lady, Miss Brown, a trained nurse, who had been with Mary all through her illness, whose cheering words did me a wonderful lot of good. One thing she said was, "Trust." God bless her!

A TESTING TIME

My old friend the Devil was in evidence during this hard time in all his pomp and glory. I could hear him say, "You see how God treats you! He don't care much or He wouldn't have taken Mary away. What did He do it for? Why, He don't know you even a little bit. Come, Dan, I'll be your friend; didn't we always have a good time together on the Bowery? Go get a 'ball'; it'll do you good and make you forget your troubles. You have a good excuse even if any one sees you." I was tempted, but I said, "Not this time, you old Devil: get behind my back!" People said, "Keep your eye on Ranney; he's up against it; now he will start to drink and go down and out."

I'm going to tell you how God came and helped me in my hour of need. It was the day of the funeral, the 17th of March, 1902. The people who were helping had gone home to get ready to attend the service, and my boy and I were left all alone with the dead. We were feeling pretty bad. My boy had lost the best friend he ever had or would have in this world. Some fathers are all right and love their children, but it isn't like a mother's love. No wonder he was weeping and feeling badly.

We were walking about the room saying nothing, just thinking, and wondering what would happen next. We happened to meet just at the head of the casket (God's doing), and stood there as though held by some unseen power, when my boy opens up like this: "Pop, you don't want me to smoke any cigarettes, do you?" I looked at him, astonished at such a question at this time, but I said, "No, Willie, I don't want you to smoke and hope you never will." Then he said, "Father, you don't want me to drink, do you?" I wondered at these questions, and looked at him with tears in my eyes. I said, "No, Bill, my poor boy, I would rather see you dead and in your coffin beside your poor mother, and know you were going to be buried to-day, than to know you would ever drink or be like your father was. Bill, don't you ever take the first glass of beer or whiskey! Ask God to keep you from it."

I wondered what was coming next, but I didn't have to wait long. The boy said, "The people are watching you and say you won't come back from the grave without having a drink, and that you won't be sober a week from now. Pop, trust in the God that saved you ten years ago, won't you? You know we promised to meet mother. Fool these people and let them see that you are the man and father I love."

I straightened up, looked at the lad, and out went my hand. We shook hands and I said, "Son, with the help of God I'll never drink again." And there at the head of the coffin we knelt and asked God to help us and make us men such as He would have us be; we asked it in the name and for the sake of the Christ who died for us.

That was March 17, 1902, and we have kept the faith up to the present time.

I'll never forget that prayer. Don't you think it pays to be on the level with God? If you ask Him to help you He will. Just trust Him and have a little backbone, and you will win out every time. I know now that this experience was God teaching me a lesson and drawing me closer to Him.

Things went differently now; I could not run the church very well alone, so after a few months I handed in my resignation. The trustees wanted me to stay, but I couldn't; sad memories would come up, and I simply had to go. I left the old church where I had spent so many happy days with a record of ten years that money could not buy. I go there once in a while even now.

THE CHURCH OF SEA AND LAND.

MIDNIGHT MISSION, CHINATOWN.

CHAPTER VII

THE MISSION IN CHINATOWN

About two years previous to my wife's death a man, Mr. H. Gould, called on me and asked me if I was the Ranney that was converted on the Bowery. I said, "Yes, I was saved about ten years ago." He said, "I've a proposal to make. I hear you are a natural-born leader of men, and I think you look it. I'm one of the trustees of the Midnight Mission in Chinatown. It's a hard place, but will you come and take charge of it? I can't keep any one there longer than a few weeks; they get drunk or are licked or done up some way. I want some one with backbone; will you take it?" I thanked him. He had said enough to make any one refuse a job like that, but I knew all the ins and outs of that quarter, and I thought I'd like the work. I asked God's guidance, and I spoke with Mr. Dennison, the pastor of the Church of Sea and Land, and he said it was wonderful the way God was leading me. "Go and see what it's like," he said. "Try it. You can run the church also, but if you see you can't get along, give it up."

My wife and boy were planning to go on a visit to Ireland to see if it would improve her health, and when I told her of Mr. Gould's proposal she did not want me to go: she was afraid I'd get killed. But I said it would help to pass the time away until she came back. So in 1900 I took charge of the Chinatown Midnight Mission, remained there six years, and left to be a lodging-house missionary.

I well remember the first night. There sat some of the old gang. They gave me the glad hand, and asked me if I was going to be the bouncer; if so, I could count on them. I said. "Yes, I'm to be the 'main guy,' bouncer, etc." They were pleased, and gave me credit of always being on the level. I made lots of friends while there.

LEADING A MEETING

I never had to use force to keep order but once while in that Mission. I had been in charge two months or so when I got notice that the leader would not be there that night, so it was up to me to lead the meeting. I'll never forget that night. There are some things a person can't forget, and that was one of them.

It was snowing and very cold outside, and the Mission was packed with men and a few women. These poor creatures had no place to go, no home; they were outcasts, there through various sins, but mostly through love of rum. I hoped some visitor would come in and I would get him to lead, but no one came, and it was up to me to give the boys a talk. I had never forgotten my first sermon at the church, so, asking God to help me, I went on the platform. I read the story of the Prodigal Son. That was easy; the hard part was to come later on. I asked if some one would play the piano, and a young fellow came up that looked as though he hadn't had a meal or slept in a bed in a month, but when he touched the keys I knew he was a master. I found out later that he was a prodigal, had left home, spent all, and was on the Bowery living on the husks.

We began by singing a hymn, after which I got up and began to talk to the men. I gave my testimony, how God had saved me from a life of crookedness and crime, and that I was no better than the worst man on the Bowery, except by the grace of God. There was one big fellow sitting in the front row who was trying to guy me. While I was talking he would make all sorts of remarks, such as, "Oh, what do you know about it? Go away back and sit down," etc. I asked him to keep still or he would have to get out. I went on trying to talk, but that man would always answer back with some foolish remark. He was trying to stop the meeting—so he told me afterwards.

There I was. I could not go on if he did, and I told him that when I got through I would give him a chance to talk. Now there were over four hundred men looking at me, wondering what I would do. Some of my old pals shouted, "Put him out, Danny!" and the meeting was in an uproar. I knew if I did not run that meeting, or if I showed the "white feather," I was done as a leader or anything else connected with that place. I said to him, "My friend, if you don't keep still I'll make an example of you." I could have called the police and had him locked up, but I didn't want any one to go behind bars and know that I had him put there. I had been there and that was enough. I've never had one of these poor men arrested in my life. I used kindness.

I began to talk again, and he started in again, but before he got many words out of his mouth I gave him a swinging upper cut which landed on the point of his jaw, lifting him about two feet, and down he went on his back. My old pals came up to help, but I said, "Sit down, men; I can handle two like that fellow." I called out a hymn; then I told him to get up, and if he thought he could behave himself he might sit down, if not, he could get out. Well, he sat down and was as good as could be.

That was the making of me. The men all saw it. They knew that I was one of them, they saw that I could handle myself, and I never had any trouble after that. And the man I hit is to-day one of my best friends.

I told the men that the Devil sent in one of his angels once in a while, the same as to-night, to disturb the meeting-place of God. I said, "You men would be a marker for God if you would only take a stand for God and cut out your sins. I never in my palmy days disturbed a meeting, drunk or sober. I always respected God's house. If I didn't like it I went out, and I think, fellows, that's one of the reasons He picked me up when I was away down in sin and made me what I am to-night. He will do the same for any one here; why not give Him a chance?"

SOMETHING NEW

This was something new for the men. Here was a man that they knew, no stranger, but one of themselves eight years before. He had been in prison with them, drunk with them, stolen with them, and in fact had done everything that they did, and now here he was telling his old pals how they could be better men, how God would help them if they would only give Him a chance.

God was with me that night. It didn't seem to be Ranney at all. I asked who wanted to get this religion, who wanted me to pray for them, and about seventy-five hands went up. A number of men came forward and took a stand for Jesus. It was early in the morning when the meeting closed. It was cold and snowing outside.

It is a hard matter to get these men to declare themselves, for they are afraid of the laugh, but I told them not to mind that; that my pals gave me the laugh when I started out. "If we are honest and have sand and help ourselves after asking God's help," I told them, "we will take no notice of a grin or a sneer. My companions wagged their heads when I started out in the new life in September, 1892. They said, 'Oh, we'll give Danny a couple of weeks. He's trying to work the missionary; he'll be back again!' Don't you men see I'm still trusting? and there isn't a man in the Mission right now that can say I'm not on the level, that I've drank whiskey or beer or done an unmanly act since I gave my life into His keeping. Why? Because I'm trusting, not in man or woman, but I'm honestly trusting in God."

I was satisfied that among the whole roomful of men there were not half a dozen that had a bed to sleep on that night. I didn't have the money to put them to bed, but I departed from the rules, and calling them to order, said, "Boys, how many of you would like to be my guest for the night?" You ought to have seen them look at me! Never such a thing had been known. It set them to thinking. The saloon-keeper wouldn't do it; what did he care for them? I said, "Boys, I'm not doing this; I don't want you to think so. It's God through me."

Many's the night after that I kept the Mission open and let the poor fellows sleep there, on the chairs and on the floor, and they appreciated it. I was winning them through kindness. When I was ready to go home to my nice warm bed, I'd read them a little riot act telling them there were always a few among a lot of men that would spoil a good thing, ending up, "Be good, boys, and have a good sleep. Good-night," and they would say so heartily, "Good-night, Danny! God bless you and keep you!"

Letting the men stay didn't cost me a cent, and there was a big fire to keep them warm and it meant much to them, poor fellows. I had the Board of Health get after me quite a few times, but I'd explain things to them, and they would go away saying, "You're all right." Big hard men said, "If people who want to do good would only get a place to house the poor unfortunates, there would be less crime and misery." I knew that was true, and I'm praying for the day when we can have just such a place, and God is going to give it in His own good time.

I had won the boys, and I stayed in that Mission over six years and saw lots of men and women saved and living good lives. Many times well-dressed men will come into my place and say, "Mr. Ranney, don't you know me?" and when I can't place them they will tell me how I was the means of saving their lives by letting them stay in out of the cold, and giving them a cup of coffee and a piece of bread in the morning. I could count them by the hundreds. Praise His name!

A POOR OUTCAST

One night just as the doors opened, there came into the Mission a woman who evidently had seen better days. She was one of the poor unfortunates of Chinatown. She asked if she might sit down, as she was very tired and did not feel well. "Go in, Anna," I said, and she went in and took a seat. When I passed her way she said, "Mr. Ranney, will you please give me a drink of water?"

Now this woman had caused me lots of trouble. She would get drunk and carry on, but when sober she would be good and feel sorry. I gave her a cup of water and she said, "Thank you, Dan, and may God bless you!" An hour after that I gave her another cup, and she thanked me again, saying, "God bless you for your patience!" The next time I looked at her she had her head on the seat in front and I thought she was sleeping. Now I never wake any sleepers. I feel that an hour's sleep will do them good, for when the Mission closes and they go out they have no place to sleep. They have to find a truck or a hallway or walk up and down the Bowery all night. I've been there, and it takes one that has been through the mill to sympathize with the "down-and-outs." So I did not disturb this woman.

The meeting was over and the people were all out, when I noticed Anna still in the same position. I went over and called her, and receiving no answer shook her a little, but she never moved. I bent over and raised her head; a pair of sightless eyes seemed to look at me, and I knew she was dead. I never had such a start in my life. Two hours before alive—now dead! I learned that she was from a town in Connecticut, of good parents, who took her to her last resting-place in the family plot—a wayward girl who ran away from home. Her "God bless you, Dan!" still rings in my ears and her dead face I'll never forget.

Here was a case that, so far as I knew, did not come under the influence of God's Spirit, and I could only say, "God have mercy on her poor soul!" but there have been scores of other women whom I have been able to reach and help by the grace of God. I shall never forget the "white slave."

RESCUED FROM A DIVE

When I had charge of the Chinatown Mission a party of three came down to see the sights and do a little slumming in the district, and they asked me to show them around. Now there wasn't a hole or joint in Chinatown or on the Bowery that I didn't know, but I didn't as a rule take women to such places. I don't like the idea of their looking at other people's misery, and there's nothing but woe and want to be seen when you go slumming. Lots of it is brought on by the people themselves, but still they are human and do not like to be looked at.

However, this night was an exception, and away we went to see the sights. I took them to the Joss House—the temple where the Chinese pray to Confucius—and other places down on Cherry Hill. But they wanted to see something hard, so I took them to a place that I thought was hard enough. If you were a stranger and went into this place and displayed a roll of "the green" you would be done up.

We went into one of the worst places on the Bowery, the women being as anxious to go as the rest. The waiter piloted us to a small round table, and we sat down and called for some soda. I'd been there before to bring out a man or a woman or a girl as the case might be, and was pretty well known as "Sky-Pilot Dan."

The party with me were astonished and wondered how such things as they saw could exist in a city like New York. There were all classes in the place, sailors, men, women, and girls, who had lost all self-respect and thought of nothing but the drink and the dance.

While sitting there the lady's attention was drawn to a girl at the next table who sat there looking at the lady, with the tears streaming down her cheeks. The lady said, "Mr. Ranney, what is the matter with that girl? Ask her to join us." I got another chair and asked the girl to come over and sit beside the lady, who asked her how she came to be there, and why she was crying.

At that the girl began to cry harder and sobbed as though her heart would break. After she became a little more quiet she said, "You look like my mother, and I'll never see her again! Oh, I wish I was dead!" We asked her why she didn't go home to her mother. She cried out, "I can't! They won't let me! And if I could get away how could I get to Cincinnati, Ohio, where my mother lives?"

We got her story from the girl, and this is how it ran: She got into conversation with a well-dressed woman in Cincinnati one day who said that she could get her a position as stenographer and typewriter at a fine salary. After telling her mother about it, she and the woman started for New York, the woman paying the fare. The woman gave her an address of a party, but when the poor girl got there, there was no job for a typewriter; it was a very different position. The young girl had been lured from home on false promises, and here she was a "white slave" through no fault of her own.

A difficult situation confronted us. The girl was in trouble and needed help, and what were we going to do about it? She was as pretty a girl as I ever saw, with large black eyes, a regular Southern type of beauty, and just beginning the downward career. That means, as the girls on the Bowery put it, first the Tenderloin, then the white lights and lots of so-called pleasure, until her beauty begins to fade, which usually takes about a year. Second, Fourteenth Street, a little lower down the grade. Third, the Bowery, still lower, where they get nothing but blows and kicks. The fourth and last step, some joint like this, the back room of a saloon, down and out, all respect gone, nothing to live for; some mother's girl picked up some morning frozen stiff; the patrol, the morgue, and then Potter's Field. Some mother away in a country town is waiting for her girl who never comes back.

God help the mothers who read this, for it's true. Look to your girls and don't trust the first strange woman who comes into your house, for she may be a wolf in sheep's clothing. She wants your daughter's fresh young beauty, that's her trade, and the Devil pays good and plenty.

I asked the girl whether she had any friends near, and she said she had an aunt living on Chestnut Street, Philadelphia, that she thought might take her. Then looking around the room she said, "But he won't let me go anyhow." I followed her look, and there standing with his back to the wall was a man I knew. Here was this young girl made to slave and earn a living for this cur! There's lots of it done in New York—well-dressed men doing no work, living on the earnings of young girls.

We got the address of the aunt in Philadelphia, and I went out and sent a message over the wire, asking if she would receive Annie if she came to Philadelphia. I received an answer in forty-two minutes saying, "Yes, send her on. I'll meet her at the station."

I hurried back, thanking God for the answer, and found them sitting at the same table. Annie was looking better than when we first met her. I said, "It's all right; her aunt will take care of her; now all we have to do is to get her to the ferry and buy her ticket."

There was a tap on my shoulder, and looking around I saw the man she had pointed out, and he said, "You want to keep your hands off that girl, Dan, or there's going to be trouble." Now I knew this kind of man; I knew he would do me if he got a chance, and he was a big fellow at that; but I thought I could hold my own with him or any of his class. I didn't mind what he said; all I was thinking about was getting the girl to Cortlandt Street Ferry.

When we got on our feet to make a start he came over and said, "She don't go out of this place; if she does there's going to be trouble." I said, "Well, if you're looking for trouble you will get all that's coming to you, and you'll get it good and plenty." And I started toward the door. He came after me, asking me what I was going to do. I said, "I'm not going to bother with you, I'm merely going to get a couple of 'Bulls'—policemen—and they will give you all the trouble you want. But that girl goes with me."

He weakened. He knew his record was bad and he did not want to go up to 300 Mulberry Street (Police Headquarters), so he said, "All right, Danny, take her, but you are doing me dirty."

We got down to the ferry all right, and the lady and I went to Philadelphia and placed Annie in her aunt's house and bid her good-by.

Frequently I get a letter from Cincinnati from Annie. She is home with her mother, and a team of oxen couldn't pull her away from home again. She writes, "God bless and keep you, Dan! I thank God for the night you found me on the Bowery!"

"TELL HER THE LATCH-STRING IS OUT"

I was in a Baptist church one Sunday night speaking before a large audience and had in the course of my talk told the above story. The meeting had been a grand one. I felt that God had been with us all the way through. I noticed one man in particular in the audience while I was telling this story. Tears were running down his cheeks and he was greatly agitated. I was shaking hands all around after the meeting was over when this man came and said, "Mr. Ranney, can I have a little talk with you?" I said, "Yes." "Wait till I get the pastor," he said, and in a few minutes the minister joined us in the vestry. The man could not speak. I saw there was something on his heart and mind, and wondered what it could be. I've had lots of men come and tell me all about themselves, how they were going to give up stealing, drinking, and all other sins, but here was something different, so I waited. He tried to speak, but could only sob. Finally he cried out with a choking sob, "Sister!" The minister's hand went out to his shoulder, mine also, and we tried to comfort him; I never saw a man in such agony. After a little he told this story:

"Mr. Ranney, I am sure God sent you here to-night. I had a lovely sister; she may be living yet; I don't know. Seventeen years ago she went out to take a music lesson, and we have never laid eyes on her since, and have never had the first line from her. Oh, if I only knew where she is! She was one of the sweetest girls you ever saw, just like the girl you spoke about to-night. She was enticed away from home by a man old enough to be her father, who left his own family to starve. I've hunted for them all over. I've never passed a poor girl on the street without giving a helping hand, always thinking of my own sweet sister, who might perhaps be in worse circumstances. Mr. Ranney, will you promise me whenever you tell that story—which I hope will be very often—just to mention that girl who left a New Jersey town some years ago? Say that mother is waiting for her daughter with arms open. Say the latch-string is out and there's a welcome. Perhaps—who can tell?—you may be the means of sending that daughter back to home and mother!"

He gave me his name and address, the girl's name also, and I promised what he wanted. Would to God this book might be the means of uniting these separated ones and sending the gray-haired mother home to heaven rejoicing! Oh, how many a mother's girl is in bondage to-night for the want of a helping hand and some kind friend to give advice!

READING ROOM, SQUIRREL INN.

MEN'S CLUB AT CHURCH OF SEA AND LAND.

CHAPTER VIII

BOWERY WORK

God moves in a mysterious way to work out His ends, and I can testify that His dealings with me have been wonderful indeed,—far beyond anything that I have ever merited. During all the years since my conversion I had always kept in touch with Dr. A. F. Schauffler, Superintendent of the City Mission and Tract Society, visiting him at his office once in a while, and he was always glad to see me. He would ask me about my work and we would have a little talk together.

LODGING-HOUSE MISSIONARY

One day I said, "Dr. Schauffler, do you know I'm a protégé of the New York City Mission?" He said, "I know it, and we have kept our eyes on you for the last ten years, and have decided to make you Lodging-House Missionary to the Bowery, if you accept."

Praise God! Wasn't it wonderful, after thirteen years of God's grace in my life, to get such an appointment! Lodging-House Missionary— I couldn't understand it! It struck me as being queer in this way; the man who under God was the means of my salvation, who was a missionary when I was converted, had resigned a few years after to become a minister, and now here was Ranney, the ex-crook and drunk, being asked to take the same position!

We don't understand God's ways and purposes; they are too wonderful for us; but here I am on the Bowery, my old stamping-ground, telling the story of Jesus and His love. And I don't believe there's a man in this big world that has a greater story to tell of God's love and mercies than I have. I'm writing this seventeen years after being saved, and I'll still say it's a grand thing to be a Christian. I would not go back to the old life for anything in the world.

Part of my work has been in Mariners' Temple, corner of Oliver and Henry Streets, Chatham Square, New York City, right on the spot where I did everything on the calendar but murder. There I could see the men every night, for we had a meeting all the year round, and every day from 1 to 2 P. M. We invited all those who were in trouble to come, and if we could help them we gladly did so. If they wanted to go to the hospital we placed them there and would do whatever we could for them, always telling them of Jesus the Mighty to save.

FROM NOTHING TO $5000 A YEAR

I remember and love a man who was my partner in the Tuesday night meetings in the Mariners' Temple, when we fed the poor fellows during the winter—a fine Christian gentleman. You would never think to look at him he was once such a drunkard! He told me his story. He had spent months hanging out in the back room of a saloon on Park Row, only going out once in a while to beg a little food. He had sold everything he could sell and he was a case to look at. He must have been, or the proprietor would never have said, "Say, you are a disgrace to this place! Get out and don't come in here again!" The poor fellow went out. He was down and out sure enough! He thought he would end it all, and he bent his steps toward the East River, intending to jump in, but was chased from the dock by the watchman.

He passed a Mission, heard the singing, and went in. He heard men that were once drunkards get up and testify to the power of God to save a man. He knew a few of the men and thought, "If God can save them He surely can me!" What a lot there is in testimony for the other fellow!

He went out that night and slept in a hallway. He waited until the Mission opened, and going in, heard the same thing again. When the invitation was given he went forward and was gloriously saved. He did not walk the street that night nor has he since. He went to work at his trade—he was a printer—and he and his dear wife, who had always prayed for her husband, were united and are now working together in the Master's vineyard.

This was over three years ago. Today this man has a position at a salary of $5000 a year! Three years ago ordered out of a Park Row saloon as a disgrace! Doesn't it pay to be a Christian and be on the level! I could go right on and tell of hundreds that have come up and are on top now. God never leaves nor forsakes us if we do our part.

The Bowery boys are queer propositions. You can't push or drive them; they will resent it and give you back as good. But if, on the other hand, you use a little tact spiced with a little kindness, you will win out with the Bowery boy every time.

It was a kind word and a kind act that were the means of saving me, and I never tire of giving the same.

A MISSIONARY IN COURT

I remember a few years ago a fellow was arrested for holding up a man on Chatham Square. Now this fellow was an ex-convict and had a very bad record, but he came to our meeting one night to see the pictures of Christ, and was so touched by them that he came again and finally raised his hand for prayers, and when the invitation was given went up to the mercy seat and was saved. At the time he was arrested he had been a grand Christian for two years.

He used to pump the organ. On this Sunday night when he was arrested I had gone over to the Chinatown Mission with him. When he left to go to his lodging-house it was 10:30, and he was arrested right after leaving the meeting on the charge of robbing a man on the Bowery at 9:30 P.M.

When he was arrested he sent for me and told me why he was arrested. Now I knew he had not robbed any one while he was with me.

The day of his trial came on. Judge Crane was the judge—a good clean man. After the man had sworn that J—— was the man who robbed him I was asked to go on the stand and tell what I knew. I told him I was a missionary to the Bowery, and that J——, the man arrested, was not the man who did the robbing, for he was with me at the time the robbery took place.

Judge Crane asked my name. I told him and gave him a brief history of my past life. He was amazed. Then I spoke a few words to the jury. The case was then given to the jury, and after twenty minutes they came in with a verdict of not guilty.

My dear readers, suppose Reilly (Ranney), the crook of sixteen years before, had been on that witness-stand. The Judge would have asked my name and when I'd said, "Reilly, the crook," they would have sent both of us off to prison for life. But the past has been blotted out through Jesus, and it was the word of the redeemed crook that set J— — free.

There are lots of cases I could write about where men are arrested and send for me. I go to the Tombs to see them, and as I go up the big stone steps where the visitors go in, the big barred gate opens, and the warden touches his hat and says, "How do you do, Mr. Ranney," and I go in. There's always a queer feeling comes over me when that gate is shut behind me. I realize that I am coming out in an hour or so, but there was a time when I was shoved through the old gate, and didn't know when I would come out.

A COUNT DISGUISED AS A TRAMP

One night in Mariners' Temple, on Chatham Square, I was leading a meeting for men; it was near closing time and the invitation had been given. There were three men at the front on their knees calling on God to help them.

I look back to that night as one I never can forget. One of the men who came up front had no coat; it had been stolen from him in some saloon while he was in a drunken sleep, so he told me. After prayer had been offered and we got on our feet we asked the men to give their testimony. In fact, I think it is a good thing for them to testify, as it helps them when they have declared themselves before the others. They each gave a short testimony in which they said that they intended to lead a better life, with God's help.

The man without a coat said he had but himself to blame for his condition, and, if God would help him, he was going to be a better man.

I saw to it that the man had a lodging and something to eat, when out from the audience stepped a fine-looking man with a coat in his hand and told the man to put it on. I looked at the man in astonishment. He was about five-feet-ten, of fine appearance, a little in need of a shave and a little water, but the man sticking out of him all over.

It is not the clothes that make the man, for here was a man who hadn't anything in the way of clothes, but you could tell by looking at him that he was a gentleman. I just stood and looked at him as he helped the other fellow on with the coat. I thought it one of the grandest acts I ever saw. He was following Christ's command about the man having two coats giving his brother one. I saw the man had on an overcoat, but, even so, it was a grand act, and I told him so.

I did not see him again for some time, when one night, about a week after the coat affair, I saw him sitting among the men at the Doyer Street Midnight Mission, of which I had charge. I went over where he was sitting and while shaking hands with him said, "Say, that was the grandest act you ever did when you gave that man your coat. What did you do it for? You don't seem to have any too much of this world's goods. How did it happen? Are you a Christian? Who are you?" He looked at me a moment and said, "Mr. Ranney, if I can go into your office I'll tell you all about it."

We went into the office, and he said, "How did you find me out?" Well, the question was a queer one to me. How did I find him out? I didn't know what he meant, but I didn't tell him so; I just smiled.

Well, he said he was a French Count (which was true), over here writing a book about the charitable institutions in the United States. He had been in Chicago, San Francisco, and in fact, all over the States, for points for his book. He told me what he had and hadn't done. He had worked in wood-yards for charity organizations; had given himself up and gone to the Island; stood in bread-lines; in fact, he had done everything the tramp does when he is "down and out."

I took quite a fancy to him. He took me up to his room in Eighteenth Street, showed me his credentials, and we became quite chummy. We used to do the slums act, and I would put on an old suit of clothes so I wouldn't be known. We would stand in the bread-line just like the rest of them and get our roll and coffee. It reminded me of my old life, and sometimes I would imagine I was "down and out" again, but it's different when you have a little change in your pocket. A dollar makes a big difference, and you can never appreciate the feelings of a poor "down and out" if you never were there yourself.

We had been going around together for about three or four weeks when one day he showed me a cable dispatch from Paris telling him he was wanted and to come at once. We had had a nice time together and I was sorry he was going.

He asked me for one of my pictures to put in his book, which I gave him. Then he wanted to know what he could do for me. I thought a moment, then said, "Give the poor fellows a feed Sunday night." I was the Sunday night leader and I wanted him on the platform. He said, "All right. Be at the Mission Sunday afternoon."

About 5 P. M. there drove up to the Mission door a carriage with a man in it who said, "Is this 17 Dover Street, and is your name Mr. Ranney?" I said, "Yes." He had four large hampers filled with sandwiches, which we carried into the Mission. He said he was the Count's valet and the Count wished him to make tea for the men. I said, "All right." I thought it would be a change for the men, although coffee would have been all right.

The tea was made and everything was ready for the feed. I wanted the papers to know about it, so I sent my assistant to the office and told the reporters that a real French Count was going to give a feed that night. They were on hand and the next day the papers all had an account of it.

As soon as the doors opened the men came in and the place was jammed to the limit. The meeting was opened with prayer, then the sandwiches and tea were passed around. The Count, wearing a dress-suit, was sitting on the platform. I introduced him as the "man of the hour" who had given the lay-out to the boys. They thanked him with three cheers.

I asked the men to look him over and see if they had ever seen him before. Now the Bowery men are sharp, and over seventy-five hands went up. They had seen him somewhere, in Mission bread-lines and different places.

The Count spoke for about five minutes and then sat down. He sailed on the following Tuesday and I never met him again. He may be in London for all I know, studying up something else. But I'm sure he enjoyed himself when feeding the men. And I have often thought, no matter who or what he was, he had his heart in the right spot. God wants men of his stamp, for He can use them for His honor and glory.

A MUSICIAN WON TO CHRIST

There isn't a week passes in my work that there are not some specially interesting happenings. One Wednesday night about six months ago we were having our usual Wednesday night meeting. I found I did not have any one to play the piano; my player had not yet come. I did not worry over that, however, as sometimes we had to go on and have a meeting without music. I generally asked if any one could play, and I did so this night. Presently a man came up the aisle. I asked, "Can you play?" He said, "A little. What number shall I play?" I said, "I guess we will sing my favorite hymn, 'When the Roll Is Called up Yonder, I'll Be There.'" He found the hymn and when he began to play I saw that he was a real musician. He made that old piano fairly talk. "Ah," said I, "here is another 'volunteer organist.'" I had seen the man and talked with him lots of times before, but always took him for a common drunkard. You can't tell what an old coat covers.

After the meeting I had a little talk with him and asked him why he was in such a condition. "Oh," he answered, "it's the old, old story, Mr. Ranney — the drink habit. I know what you are going to say: why don't I cut it out? Well, I can't. I have tried time and again. I'll go on drinking until I die." I told him to stop trying and ask God to help him, just to lean on His arm, He wouldn't let him fall. I left him thinking it over, and I kept track of him, getting in an odd word here and there and giving him food and lodging.

74

In four weeks we won out and he became a good Christian man. Now he plays at our meetings and takes a share in them, giving his testimony. I've had him over to my home many times. He takes great delight in our garden there and waits with longing for Thursday to come, for that's the day he visits us, the best one in the week for him. There's nothing like the country for building a man up.

This man came from a good German family, and can play three instruments, piano, violin, and clarinet. I asked him if he was married. "No," he answered, "thank God I never was married. I have not that sin on my soul! I've done nearly everything any one else has done: been in prison many a time, drank and walked the streets lots of nights. I've written home to my mother and told her I had taken her Jesus as mine, and, Mr. Ranney, here's a letter from her." I read the letter. It was the same old letter, the kind those loving mothers write to their wayward boys, thanking God that she lived to see her boy converted and telling him the door was always open, and for him to come home. How many mothers all over the world are praying for their boys that they have not seen for years, boys who perhaps are dead or in prison! God help those mothers!

SAVED THROUGH AN OUTDOOR MEETING

Part of my work consists in holding outdoor meetings. Through my friend Dan Sullivan I received a license for street preaching, so whenever an opportunity opens I speak a word for the Master, sometimes on a temporary platform, sometimes standing on a truck, and sometimes from the Gospel Wagon. It is "in season and out of season," here, there, and everywhere, if we are to get hold of the men who don't go near the churches or even the missions.

One night while holding an outdoor meeting on the Bowery at Bleecker Street, I was speaking along the line of drink and the terrible curse it was, how it made men brutes and all that was mean, telling about the prodigal and how God saved him and would save to the uttermost. There were quite a number of men around listening.

The meeting ended and we had given all an invitation to come into the Mission. One young man, well dressed, came up to me and, taking my hand, said he believed every word I said. I saw at a glance he was not of the Bowery type. I got to talking to him and asked him into the Mission. He said he had never been into a place like that in his life and did not take any stock in them, but my talk had interested him. He could not understand how I had given up such a life as I said I had led and had not taken a drink in sixteen years. I said I had not done this in my own strength, but that God had helped me win out, and that God would help any one that wanted to be helped.

We got quite friendly and he told me all about himself. He had just got his two weeks' salary, which amounted to $36.00. He was married and had two sweet little children and a loving wife waiting for him uptown. He told me he had taken a few drinks, as I could plainly see, and he was going down to see the Bowery and do a little sight-seeing in Chinatown. I knew if he went any further he would be a marker for the pickpocket or others and would know nothing in a little while, so I tried to get him into the Mission, and after quite a while succeeded, and we took a seat right by the door. He was just tipsy enough to fall asleep, and I let him do it, for a little sleep often does these men a great deal of good, changing all their thoughts when they wake. When he woke the testimonies were being given. I rose to my feet and gave my testimony, and sat down again. The invitation came next, for all those that wanted this Jesus to stand. I tried to get him on his feet, but he would not take a stand; still the seed had been sown.

He told me where he was working and where he lived—wrote it down for me. He was bent on going, so I said I would go up to the corner with him. He wanted one more drink—the Devil's temptation!—but at last I coaxed him to the Elevated Station at Houston Street. He said, "I wish you could see my home and family. Will you come up with me?" It was 10 P. M. and going would mean home for me about the early hours. But I went up to the Bronx, got to his home, saw him in, was bidding him good-night; nothing would do but I should come in. He had a nice little flat of five rooms. I was introduced to his wife, who was a perfect lady. He wanted to send out for beer. I objected, and his wife said, "George, don't drink any more! I think you have had enough."

Now was the time for me to get in a little of God's work, so I told him my life, and what drink did for me, and I had an attentive audience. When I finished, his wife said, "I wish my husband would take your Jesus, Mr. Ranney. I'm a Christian, but, oh, I'd give anything if George would take Christ and give up his drinking!" He made all kinds of objections and excuses, but we pleaded and prayed. God was working with that man, and at 3 o'clock in the morning we knelt down, the wife, the husband and I, way up in the Bronx, and God did mightily save George. He went to his business on Monday sober. That was three years ago, and he has held out well. He has been advanced twice, with a raise in salary, and comes down to help me in my work on the Bowery. God has blessed him wonderfully, and He will any one who has faith to believe.

JIM THE BRICKLAYER

Where I meet so many men every day and have so many confessions and try to lend a helping hand in so many places, I do forget some of the men, for it seems as though there was an endless procession of them through the Bowery. But some cases stand out so prominently that I shall never forget them. I remember one man in particular who used to come into the Mission. He was one of the regulars and was nearly always drunk. He used to want us to sing all the time. He was a fine fellow, but down and out, and every cent he could earn went to the saloons. I would talk to him nearly every night and ask him why he did not stop his drinking. He would listen, but the next night he would be drunk just the same.

There was good stuff in him, for he was a good bricklayer and could make from $5.00 to $6.00 per day. He told me he was married, and his wife and two children were in Syracuse, living perhaps on charity, while he, instead of making a living for them and giving them a good home, was here on the Bowery drinking himself to death.

He would often say, "Danny, if I could only sober up and be a man and go back to my family, I'd give anything. But what's the use of trying? I can't stop, and I wish sometimes that I was dead. And sometimes, Mr. Ranney, I'm tempted to end it all in the river."

I reasoned with this man time and time again, but with no effect. He knew it was the right way to live, but thought it was not for him, and I thought that if a man was ever gone it was that young man.

One night as the invitation was being given I caught his eye and I said, "Jim, come up front and get rid of that drink." But he said, "What's the use?" I went down, took him by the hand, led him up front, and we all knelt down and asked God to save these poor men. I asked them all to pray for themselves and when I got to Jim I said, "Jim, now pray." And he said, "Lord, help me to be a man and cut the 'booze' out of my life for Jesus' sake. Amen."

He meant business that night and was as sincere as could be. We all got up from our knees, and I put the usual question to them all, now that they had taken Jesus, what were they going to do? It came Jim's turn, and he said, "Mr. Ranney, I've asked God to help me, and I'm going out of this Mission and I'm not going to drink any more whiskey." Then almost in the same breath he said, "I wonder if God will give me a pair of pants." That created a smile in the audience. I knew I could get Jim a pair of pants, and he needed them badly. Just imagine a man six feet tall with a pair of pants on that reached just below the knees, and you have Jim.

I said, "Jim, you have asked God to help you, and He will if you let him. If you keep sober until Friday night, and come in here every night and give your testimony, no matter how short, God will send you a pair of pants." This was on Monday night, my own special night. I knew if Jim came in every night sober, something was doing. Tuesday night came, and sure enough there was Jim with his testimony. He got up and thanked God for being one day without taking a drink. I said, "Praise God! Keep it up, Jim!" Wednesday night Jim thanked God for two days' victory. He was doing finely. Thursday came, and Jim was there with his testimony of three days saved. He had one more day to go before he got his pants. Friday night came and I had gone up and got the pants, but no Jim made his appearance. Near closing time the door opened and in walked Jim. He stood back and just roared out, "Danny, I'm as drunk as a fool; I've lost the pants!" then walked out.

I did not see him for a couple of nights, then he came into the Mission, sat down and was fairly quiet. I reached him in the course of the evening and shook hands with him, but I did not say a word about his going back. That worried him a good deal, for he said, "Dan, are you mad with me?" I said, "No, Jim, I'm mad with the Devil, and I wish I could kick him out of you and kill him." Jim smiled and said, "You're a queer one."

I did not give Jim up, but I did not say anything to him about giving up the drink again for about a week. He would always be in the meeting and I would notice him with a handshake and a smile. I could see he was thinking quite hard and he was not drinking as much as he had been. I was praying for that man, and I was sure that He was going to give me Jim.

One night about a month after Jim had tried the first time, I was giving the invitation to the men, as usual, for all who wanted this salvation to come forward and let us pray with them. After coaxing and pleading with them there were six fellows that came forward and knelt down, when to my astonishment who came walking up the aisle but Jim! He knelt down with the others and prayed. I did not know what the prayer was, but when he rose he went back and took his seat and said nothing.

A month went by to a day. There were testimonies every night from all over the Mission about what God had done and was doing, but Jim never gave the first word of testimony. I often wondered why. This night he got on his feet, and this is what he said: "Men, I've been everything that's bad and mean, a crook and a drunkard, separated from wife and children, a good-for-nothing man. I want to stand here before you people and thank God for keeping me for one whole month; and, men, this is the happiest month I've spent in my life. I asked God to help me and He is doing so. I only wish some of you men would take Jesus as your friend and keeper the same as I have. I'm going to stick, with God's help. I want you Christian people to keep on praying for me, as I feel some one has," and he sat down. Oh, how I did thank God for that testimony! You know a person can tell the true ring of anything, gold, silver, brass, everything, and I knew the ring of that testimony.

Jim stayed after the meeting and we talked things over pretty well. He was a mechanic, but his tools were in pawn. I said, "Jim, I'll meet you to-morrow and we will go and get your tools out." In the morning Jim and I went down to the pawnbroker in New Chambers Street, and Jim produced the tickets, paid the money due, with interest, and received his stock in trade, the tools.

The next thing was a job. I knew a boss mason who was putting up a building in Catherine Street. We saw the boss and he took Jim on. He went to work and made good. He would always come and see me at night, and always testify to God's keeping power. He would ask me, "Do you think I can get back to my wife and children again?" "Yes," I would answer; "wait a little while. Have you written to her?" "Yes." "Got any answer?" "Yes, a couple of letters, but I don't think she takes any stock in my conversion. Dan, can't we have our pictures taken together? I have written my wife a lot about you. I told her you were worse than I ever was. Perhaps if she sees our faces and sees how I look, she may think of old times and give me one more chance."

Jim had been four months converted at this time, and God had him by the hand. It was great to see that big strong man, like a little child in God's love. We went out and had our pictures taken and Jim asked me to write and urge his wife to give him one more chance. I did as Jim wanted me; in fact, I wrote her about everything he said and enclosed the picture.

Every night Jim would come around with the question, "Danny, any word from up State yet?" "Not yet, Jim: have a little patience, she will write soon." We finally got the longed-for letter, but it wasn't favorable. Among other things she said she took no stock in her husband, and that she knew he was the same old good-for-nothing, etc. It was hard lines for poor Jim, who was reading that letter over my shoulder. I looked at him. I could see some of the old Devil come into his eyes. The wife little knew what an escape Jim had then and there. I cheered him up and we got on our knees and prayed good and hard, and God heard the prayer and Jim was sailing straight once more and trusting Jesus.

A thought flashed through my mind, and I said, "Jim, have you any money?" "Yes," he said, "I have over sixty dollars." He gave me the money and we went to the postoffice and I took out a money-order to Mrs. Jim, Syracuse, N. Y., for sixty dollars and sent it on signed by Jim and took the receipt and put it in my pocket.

Five days after I was sitting at my desk in the Mission. A knock came to the door. I said, "Come in," and a woman with two little girls entered. I placed a chair and waited. She said, "You are Mr. Ranney. I recognize you from your picture." She was Jim's wife, as she told me. Then she began about her troubles with her husband: he was a good man, but he would drink. She said, "I begin to think that Jim has religion, for if he hadn't something near it, he would never have sent me the money. Do you think he is all right, Mr. Ranney?" To which I answered that I really believed he was, and that he would be a good husband and father. I asked her if she was a Christian, and she said, "Yes, I go to church and do the best I can." I told her going to church was a good thing, but to have Jesus in your heart and home is a better one.

ONE OF MR. RANNEY'S OPEN-AIR MEETINGS.

She wanted to see Jim, so we went round to where he was working. There he was up four stories laying front brick. I watched him, so did his wife. Finally I put my hands like a trumpet and called, "Hello, Jim!" Jim looked down, seeing me, and then looking at the woman and children a moment he dropped everything, and to watch that man come down that ladder was a sight. He rushed over, threw his arms around his wife, then took the little girls in his arm, and what joy there was! There was no more work that day.

Jim showed her the saloons he used to get drunk in, and he did not forget to show the place where he was converted, and on that very spot we all had a nice little prayer-meeting, and as a finale, Mrs. Jim took Jesus, saying, "If He did all that for Jim, I want Him too."

They are back in Syracuse, living happily. Jim has a class of boys in the Sunday-school and is a deacon in the church. I had the pleasure of eating dinner in their home. I often get a letter from Jim, telling of God's goodness. He says he will never forget the fight he made for the pants or his friend Danny Ranney.

CHAPTER IX

PRODIGAL SONS

A CESSPOOL

The Bowery has always been a notorious thoroughfare. Twenty years ago there were few places in the world that for crime, vice and degradation could be compared with it. Many changes for the better have taken place in the last few years, however. Following the Lexow Commission investigation, scores of the worst haunts of wickedness were closed and vice became less conspicuous. The Bowery, however, still maintains its individuality as a breeding-place of crime. It is still the cesspool for all things bad. From all over the world they come to the Bowery. The lodging-houses give them cheap quarters, from 7 cents to 50 cents per night. These places shelter 30,000 to 40,000 men and boys nightly, to breathe a fetid and polluted air. Those who have not the price—and God knows they are many—homeless and weary, "about ready to die," sleep in hallways, empty trucks, any place for a lie-down.

Some of the lodging-houses are fairly respectable and run on a good scale, and others are the resort of the lowest kind of human outcasts. On one floor, the air poisoned beyond description, the beds dirty, will be found over a hundred men, of all classes, from the petty thief to the Western train-wrecker, loafers, drug-fiends, perhaps a one-time college man, who through the curse of drink has got there. But they are not all bad on the Bowery. No one not knowing the conditions can imagine what a large class there is who would work if they could get it, but once down it's hard to get up. A few weeks of this life wrecks them and makes old men of them. No one but God can help them, and most of them go down to early graves unknown.

A REMARKABLE DRUNKARD

I knew once one of the best lawyers of his day, living here a little off Chatham Square, in a lodging-house, brought there through rum. I've known men, lawyers, coming to see this man and getting his opinion on legal matters. He had many such visitors in his room, but he wasn't worth anything unless he was about half full of whiskey. These men would know that. They would bring a couple bottles of the stuff, as though for a social time, and then ask him questions pertaining to the case in hand. Then he would imagine himself the lawyer of old days, and plead as he saw the case, and he was right nine times out of ten! Oh, what a future that man had thrown away for the Devil's stuff, rum! Those lawyers would go away with advice from that man worth thousands of dollars, bought with a few bottles of whiskey. He told me he had left his wife and family to save them from shame. He has sons and daughters in good standing. They never see him want for anything and pay his room-rent yearly, only he must not go near them.

FORGIVING FOR CHRIST'S SAKE

Where I am located at this writing, at the Squirrel Inn, No. 131 Bowery, is a grand place for my work. I come in touch with all classes, and when I see a man or a boy that I think will stick, I rig him up, put a front on him and back him until he gets work. I wish I had more clothes so I could help more men, but at least I can give them a handshake, a kind word, and a prayer, and that, by God's grace, can work wonders for the poor fellows. There's not a man or boy comes in that I do not see, and I mingle with them and get their hard-luck stories, also their good-luck ones. Sitting there at my desk, I glance down the room, and I can tell at a glance the newcomers and the regulars. I can tell what has brought them there.

Over at one of the tables trying to read sat one day a man about fifty, his clothes worn and threadbare, but wearing a collar, and that's a good sign. I beckoned him to come over to me and I pointed to a chair, telling him to sit down. If that chair could only speak, what a tale it could tell of the men who have sat there and told their life stories!

I asked him how he came to be there, and he told me the same old story that can be summed up in one word—drink! He came from up the State, at one time owned a farm outside of Oswego, and was living happily. He was a church member and bore a good name. "I used to take an odd drink, but always thought I could do without it," said he. "Eighteen years ago I lost my wife and to drown my sorrow I got drunk. I had never been intoxicated before, and I kept at it for over three months, and when I began to come to myself, I was told that I had to get out of my home. I couldn't understand it, but I was told I had sold my farm and everything I owned for a paltry $200 to a saloon-keeper, who I thought was my dearest friend!

"That happened eighteen years ago, and I've been pretty near all over the world since then, sometimes hungry, sometimes in pretty good shape, but I'll never forget that saloon-keeper. I'll see him again, and he will pay for what he did!"

I gave that man a ticket for lodging and a couple of meals. We talked about his early life, and I asked why he didn't start out and be a Christian and not harbor a grudge; to let God punish that saloon-keeper. I told him I'd been through something like the same experience, a man whose word I trusted selling me some Harbor Chart stock and making me think he was doing me a good turn, and I lost several hundred dollars. That was in the years when I first started to be a Christian. I had the hardest time to forgive this man, but thank God I did!

I reasoned with that man day after day and saw that the light was breaking in his heart. Weeks went on, and he came to a point where he took Jesus as his guide and friend, and to-day he is a fine Christian gentleman. I have had him testifying in the church to the power of Christ to save a man. He tells me he has forgiven that saloon-man for Christ's sake.

SAVED ON THE THRESHOLD OF VICE

One afternoon about 5 o'clock I was sitting at my desk at the Mission Room when I noticed among the men who came there to read and rest and perhaps take a nap, a young man, a boy rather, clean and wearing good clothes. I looked at him a moment and thought, "He has got into the wrong place." I spoke to him, as is my habit, and asked him what he was doing there. I brought him over and got him to sit down in that old chair where so many confessions are made to me and said kindly, "Well, what's your story?" I thought of my own boy, and my heart went out to this young fellow.

He said, "You are Mr. Ranney. I've often heard about you, and I'm glad to see you now." He told me how he had given up his job on Eighth Avenue around 125th Street the day before. He had had a "run in," as he called it, at home, and had determined to get out. His mother had married a second time, and his stepfather and he could not agree on a single thing. He loved his mother, but could not stand the stepfather. He had drawn his pay at the jewelry store where he was working and had spent the night before at a hotel uptown, intending to look for a job the next day.

He had risen at 8 A. M. intending to get work before his eight dollars was all gone. Well, the money was burning a hole in his pocket. He wanted to see a show and he came down on the Bowery and got into a cheap vaudeville show, and quite enjoyed himself. "I came out of that show," he said, "and went into a restaurant to eat, and when I went to pay the cashier I did not have a cent in my pocket. The boss of the place said that was an old story. He was not there to feed people for nothing. I said I had been robbed or lost my money somehow, but he wouldn't believe me. He wanted his twenty cents, or he would have me arrested. Oh, he was mad for fair, Mr. Ranney. He got me by my coat-collar and shook me and said I was a thief, and he finished up by kicking me through the door, and here I am down on the Bowery homeless."

Another young fellow gone wrong! Could I help him? I urged him to go back home, but he didn't want to. The night before was pay-night, and he was always expected to give in his share towards the home expenses, and now here was his money all gone. What could he do?

I took him around the room and pointed out the hard cases there, wretched, miserable specimens of men, and asked him if he wanted to be like them, as he surely would if he went on in the course he was starting. He said, "Indeed I don't!" "Well, then," I said, "take my advice and go home. Be a man and face the music. It will mean a scolding from your father, but take it. Tell them both that you will make up the money as soon as you get work, and that you are going to be obedient and good from now on."

At last he said he would go if I would go with him, but I couldn't that night, for I had a meeting to address. I told him I would give him a lodging for the night, and we would go up to Washington Heights the next day. I put him in about as tough a lodging as I could get, for I wanted him to realize the life he would drift into, told him to meet me at one o'clock the next day, and said good-night to him.

The next day I met him; we had something to eat, and I asked him how he had slept. "Oh," he said, "it was something awful! I could not sleep any, there was such a cursing and drinking and scrapping. Oh, I wish I was home!"

We went up to Washington Heights, around 165th Street, and found the place. We got there about six o'clock. I went in and knocked at the door, which opened very quickly. The mother and father came forward; they had been crying, I could see that. "Oh, has anything happened to my boy!" she cried, when I asked if she had a son. "Tell me quick, for God's sake!" I told them that Eddie was all right, and I called to him. He came in, and like a manly boy, after kissing his mother, he turned to his stepfather and said, "Forgive me; I'll be a better boy and I'll make everything all right when I get a job. This is Mr. Ranney, the Bowery missionary." I went in and was asked to stay for supper, and we had an earnest talk, leading to the father giving up beer. What he was going to drink for supper was thrown into the sink. I see these people occasionally, and they are doing well.

THE PRODIGAL SON ON THE BOWERY

Here is a picture story of a boy who left home and took his journey to the "far country." It is a true story.

Away up in northern New York there is a rich man whose family consists of a wife, two sons and a daughter, all good church members. It is of the younger boy I want to speak. He is a little wayward, but good at heart, and would do anything to help any one.

Now, there has lately come back from New York a young man who has started the drink habit. This man is telling all about New York, what a grand place it is, and, if a fellow had a little money, he could make a fortune. He succeeds in arousing the fancies of this young boy, and he believes all the fellow says. People up the State look on a man as sort of a hero because he has been to New York.

Tom thinks he would like to go to the city, and when he gets home he broaches the subject to his mother. He says, "I'll get a job and make a man of myself." The mother tells him he had better stay at home and perhaps later on he would have a chance to start a business in the village where he was born. No, nothing but New York will do for him. He teases his father and mother nearly to death, until his father says, "Well, my boy, if you will, you will." Then he gives him a couple hundred dollars and a letter to a merchant whom he knows.

Tom packs his valise and is all ready to start. I can see the mother putting a Testament into her boy's hand and telling him to read it once a day and be sure to write home often. Oh, he promises all right, and is anxious to get away in a hurry. I can see them in the railroad station when the mother takes him to her bosom and kisses him. There's a dry choking in the father's throat when he bids him good-by—and then the train is off!

Now, Tom has a chum in New York, so at the first station at which they stop he gets off and sends a telegram to his friend, saying: "Ed, I'm coming on the 2.30 train. Meet me at the Grand Central Station." You may be sure Ed meets him at the station—Ed is not working—and he gives him the hello and the glad hand. He takes Tom's grip and they start for the hotel. I can see them going into a saloon and having a couple of beers, then going to the hotel, getting a room and supper, and having a good time at the theatre and elsewhere.

Time goes on. Two hundred doesn't last long. I can see Ed shaking Tom when the money is running low. I can see Tom counting the little he has left and going to a furnished room at $1.50 a week. Tom is beginning to think and worry a bit. He has lost the letter to the merchant his father gave him, and he doesn't know where to find him. No wonder he is down in the mouth! He looks for work, but can't get anything to do.

Now, all he has to do is to write home and tell his father the facts, and he will send back a railroad ticket. But Tom is proud, and he hasn't reached the point where, like the prodigal, he says, "I will arise and go to my father." No, he has not as yet reached the end of his rope. I can see him pawning the watch and chain given him by his parents. This tides him over for a little while. When that money is gone, his overcoat goes, and, in fact, everything he has is gone.

He goes down and down, and finally reaches the Bowery, where they all go in the end. He is down and out, without a cent in his clothes, walking the streets night after night—-"carrying the banner." Sometimes he slips into a saloon where they have free lunch and picks up a piece of bread here and a piece of cheese there. Sometimes he is lucky to fill in on a beef stew, but very seldom.

Now, if that isn't living on husks, I don't know what you call it! His clothes are getting filthy and he is in despair. How he wishes he had never left home! He hasn't a friend in the big city, and he doesn't know which way to turn. He says, "I'll write home." But no, he is too proud. He wants to go home the same as he left it. And the longer he waits the worse he will be. No one grows any better, either bodily or morally, by being on the Bowery. So the quicker they go to some other place the better.

But the Bowery draws men by its own strange attraction. They get into the swing of its life, and find the company that misery loves. God knows there's plenty of it there! I've seen men that you could not drive from the Bowery. But when a man takes Jesus as his guide he wants to search for better grounds.

Well, Tom had hit the pace that kills. And one night—about five years ago—there wandered into the Mission where I was leading a meeting a young man with pale cheeks and a look of utter despair on his face, looking as though he hadn't had a square meal in many a day. It was Tom. I didn't know him then. There are so many such cases on the Bowery one gets used to them. But I took particular notice of this young man. He sat down and listened to the services, and when the invitation was given to those who wanted to lead better lives he put up his hand.

Now there was something striking about his face, and I took to him. I thought of my own life and dreaded the future for him. I spoke to him, gained his confidence by degrees, and he told me his story as written in the preceding pages.

Here was a prodigal just as bad as the one in the Bible story. Well, he was converted that night and took Jesus as his helper. He told me all about his home, mother, and friends who had enough and to spare. The servants had a better time and more to eat than he. "Tom," I said, "why don't you go home?" "Oh, Mr. Ranney," he said, "I wish I could, but I want to go back a little better than I am now." And God knows he was in bad shape; the clothes he had on you couldn't sell to a rag-man; in fact, he had nothing!

I pitied the poor fellow from my heart. I was interested. I got his father's address and sat down and wrote him a letter telling him about his son's condition, etc. In a few days I received a letter from his father inclosing a check for $10, and saying, "Don't let my son starve; do all you can for him, but don't let him know his father is doing this."

Can't you see plainly the conditions? Our Father in heaven stands ready at all times to help, but we must do something—meet the conditions. Tom's father was ready to forgive and take him back, but he wanted Tom to make the surrender.

I looked after Tom to a certain extent, but I wanted him to learn his lesson. There were times when he walked the streets and went hungry. I corresponded with his father and told him how his son was getting along. I got Tom a job washing dishes in a restaurant—the Bowery's main employment—at $2.50 per week, and he stuck.

I watched him closely. He would come to the Mission nearly every night and would stand up and testify to God's goodness. He was coming on finely. Many's the talk we would have together about home. The tears would come to his eyes and he would say, "Oh, if I ever go home I'll be such a different boy! Do you think father will forgive me, Mr. Ranney?"

Well, eight months went on, and I thought it was time to get him off the Bowery—he had had his lesson. So I wrote his father, and he sent the necessary cash for clothes, railroad ticket, etc. And one night I said, "Tom, would you like to go home?" You can imagine Tom's answer! I took him out and bought him clothes, got back his watch and chain from the pawnbroker, and went with him to the Grand Central Station. I got his ticket, put him on the train, said "Good-by and God bless you!" and Tom was bound for home.

I receive a letter from him every month or so. I have visited his home and have been entertained right royally by his father and mother. I visited Tom last summer, and we did have a grand time fishing, boating, driving, etc. I asked him, "Do you want to go back to New York, Tom?" and he smiled and said, "Not for mine!" If any one comes from New York and happens to say it's a grand place to make your fortune, Tom says, "New York is a grand place to keep away from." You couldn't pull him away from home with a team of oxen.

"He arose and went to his father." Tom fed on husks. He learned his lesson—not too dearly learned, because it was a lasting one. He is now a man; he goes to church and Sunday-school, where he teaches a class of boys. Once in a while he rings in his own experience when he was a prodigal on the Bowery and far from God, and God's loving-kindness to him.

There are other boys on the Bowery from just as good families as Tom's—college men some of them—who are without hope and without God's friendship or man's. What can you and I do for them?

LAST WORDS

I have married again, and have a good sweet Christian as companion, and we have a little girl just beginning to walk. I'm younger, happier, and a better man in mind and body than I was twenty years ago. I've a good home and know that all good things are for those that trust.

I remember one night, when I was going home with my wife, I met a policeman who had arrested me once. He had caught me dead to rights—with the goods. After awaiting trial I got off on a technical point. I said, "Helen, let me introduce you to the policeman that arrested me one time." He had changed some; his hair was getting gray. He knew me, and when I told him I was a missionary, he said, "God bless you, Reilly" (that's the name I went under), "and keep you straight! You did cause us fellows a lot of trouble in those days."

Indeed I did cause trouble! There wasn't a man under much closer watch than I was twenty years ago. Just one incident will illustrate this and show what a change God brings about in a man's life when he is soundly converted. It was in 1890 that a pal of mine and I were told of a place in Atlantic City where there was any amount of silverware, etc., in a wealthy man's summer home, so we undertook to go there and see if we could get any of the good things that were in the house. We reached the city with our kit of tools, and my pal went and hid them a little way from the station, waiting till night, as we did not want to carry them around with us. Tom said, "Dan, I'm hungry; I'll go and see what I can get in a bakery." We were not very flush and could not afford anything great in the way of a dinner. Off he went, and I was to wait till he came back.

I sat down in the waiting-room, when a man came up and sat down beside me, giving me a good-day. "Nice weather," said he. I said, "Yes." Said he, "How's little old New York?" "All right," I answered. "Have you got your ticket back?" said he. I thought he was a little familiar, and I said, "It's none of your business." He was as cool as could be. "Oh, yes," he said, "it is my business," and turning the lapel of his coat he held a Pinkerton badge under my nose, at the same time saying, "The game's called, and I know you. Where's the tools?" I told him I did not have any. "The only thing that saves you," said he. "Now you get out of here when that next train goes, or there will be a little trouble." My pal came in at this time, and I winked at him to say nothing. He understood. We took that train all right, and lost our tools.

I never saw Atlantic City again until 1908, when I was asked to speak at the Y. M. C. A. I told this story in my talk. I've been back four times; I've been entertained at one of the best hotels there, the Chalfonte, for a week at a time. What a change! Twenty years ago, when I was in the Devil's employ, run out of town; now, redeemed by God, an invited guest in that same place. See what God can do for a man!

It's a hard thing to close this record of the grace of God in my life, for I feel as though I was leaving a lot of friends. If at any time you are on the Bowery—not down and out—and want to see me, why, call at No. 131, the Squirrel Inn Mission and Reading Room, and you'll find a hearty welcome.

Printed in the United Kingdom
by Lightning Source UK Ltd.
125860UK00001B/464/A

9 781406 542073